# THE SIMPLE SQUEEZE

# IN BRIDGE

by Frank Schuld

DRAKE PUBLISHERS INC.    NEW YORK

## DEDICATED

*to DIANA, my wife,*

*and favorite bridge partner.*

Published in 1974 by
Drake Publishers Inc.
381 Park Avenue South
New York, N.Y. 10016

Library of Congress Cataloging in Publication Data

Schuld, Frank P.
    The simple squeeze in bridge.

    1. Contract bridge.   I.   Title.
GV1282.3.S38      795. 4'15      74-6305
ISBN  O-87749-694-3
ISBN  0-87749-695-1   (pbk.)


Printed in The United States of America

# TABLE OF CONTENTS

# INTRODUCTION

In answer to the question, do you play bridge, about forty million people in the United States would answer in the affirmative. Actually, 90% of this number have only a cursory knowledge of the mechanics of the game and play infrequently. While the other two million compete on a more regular basis, only a small fraction of them enjoy any degree of proficiency at the game. It is from this diminutive but elite group that your top tournament and money bridge players evolve.

Why is it that the same names appear and reappear as winners in top flight competition? The answer is simple. Not only do they bid each hand with a greater measure of accuracy and partnership understanding, but they also play their cards out both as Declarer and on defense with the highest degree of technical competency.

If you wish to become more than just another mediocre bridge player, mastering the techniques of the Squeeze Play is an absolute requirement. Contrary to popular belief, executing a squeeze does not require exceptional abilities. You, the intermediate player, can develop the skills necessary to effect just such an advanced play.

The single squeeze or simple squeeze, as it is sometimes called, represents the vast majority of all squeeze situations with which the average player is likely to be confronted. The small remainder are the rare and exotic squeeze situations that are often discovered only after the hand has been played and a post-mortem analysis performed.

Almost all bridge knowledge can be acquired through practical experience. This is not true of the squeeze. The mechanics involved run contrary to a bridge player's very nature. Therefore, it is best to acquire the principles of squeeze play through study before applying them during play, and, believe me, there is nothing to match that "once in a lifetime thrill" that comes from planning and executing your first squeeze.

Most of us do not enjoy a retention rate that is equal to our reading speed. If you have had little or no experience with squeeze play, it is unlikely you will be able to understand and remember everything contained in this text at your first reading. I suggest you try to absorb its contents a little at a time, going back and re-reading those parts which give you the most difficulty.

### A Word About the Bidding

An auction is shown with every deal. It may serve only as the vehicle by which the partnership bid or misbid their way to the final contract, but it may also contain clues to be used in making a decision on the selection of a line of play. In no way do I wish to be held personally responsible for some of the auctions.

# Chapter I

# The Basic Squeeze and The BLUE Law

## What is a Squeeze

The cards in a defender's hand can be divided into two general categories, BUSY cards and IDLE cards. BUSY cards are working cards. They serve useful purposes as winners, anticipated winners, stoppers, guards, et al. IDLE cards are non-working cards. They either serve no useful purpose or duplicate a function already being performed by the defenders' partner. IDLE cards may be used as free discards when the need arises.

## Definition

When a defending hand no longer contains an IDLE card, it can be forced to release a BUSY card. If this discard provides Declarer with a winner to which he would not normally be entitled, the defender has been SQUEEZED.

```
                    NORTH
                    ♠
                    ♡ 8
                    ◇
        WEST        ♣ Q6        EAST
        ♠ Q                     ♠ 9
        ♡                       ♡ Q 10
        ◇                       ◇
        ♣ J 9       SOUTH       ♣
                    ♠ J
                    ♡ K
                    ◇
                    ♣ 10
```

1

In Illustration (A) East's cards have no defensive value. They are said to be Idle cards. West, on the other hand, holds nothing but Busy cards. Each of his remaining three cards serves as a stopper or as a guard card. None of these functions can be taken over by co-defender, West.

As South plays the ♥ K, West is faced with a choice of equally unpleasant discards. He may play his ♠ Q, which establishes South's ♠ J, or he may pitch a club, which permits Declarer to win the two remaining tricks with Dummy's ♣ Q 6.

West has been squeezed.

Notice what happens if we transpose the East and West card holdings.

NORTH

♠
♡ 8
◊
♣ Q6

WEST

♠ 9
♡ Q 10
◊
♣

EAST

♠ Q
♡
◊
♣ J 9

SOUTH

♠ J
♡ K
◊
♣ 10

As you see here, the play of the ♥ K produces the same result should East happen to be the defender who holds the Busy cards in spades and clubs. If a Squeeze is equally effective against either opponent it is said to be an AUTOMATIC Squeeze.

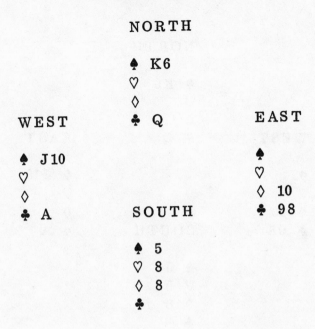

NORTH

♠ K6
♡
◊
♣ Q

WEST

♠ J10
♡
◊
♣ A

EAST

♠
♡
◊ 10
♣ 98

SOUTH

♠ 5
♡ 8
◊ 8
♣

In Illustration (C) East's ◆ 10 is a Busy card. It defends against South's ◆ 8, but this cannot stop us from developing a Spade-Club Squeeze against his partner. West holds all Busy cards. His ♣ A protects against North's ♣ Q, while his ♣ J 10 guard against dummy's ♣ K 6. Neither of these knctiof can be taken over by his partner. As South plays his last mp, the ♥ 8, West t part with either the ♣ A or one of his spades. The choices are equally distasteful. An extra trick must be forfeited to declarer.

West has been squeezed.

NORTH

♠ K6
♡
◇
♣ Q

WEST                               EAST

♠                                  ♠ J 10
♡                                  ♡
◇ 10                               ◇
♣ 98          SOUTH                ♣ A

♠ 5
♡ 8
◇ 8
♣

As you see, the squeeze is not equally effective against a Busy East. South plays the ♥ 8. Dummy must discard before, not after, the Busy defender, East. If the ♣ Q is played, East's ♣ A becomes an Idle card and can be used as a free discard. If a small spade is pitched from the table, East will follow suit.

If the defending hands cannot be freely interchanged, the success or failure of the squeeze depends upon the *position* of the Busy opponent. The Squeeze is therefore said to be a POSITIONAL SQUEEZE.

The Squeeze positions described in Illustrations (A) and (C) were not accidental. They did not just happen. These end situations were brought about by a knowledgeable declarer who employed his skills at the squeeze play. When the proper conditions exist, or are caused to exist, through the use of proper squeeze techniques, a squeeze will occur with the same inexorable precision as death and taxes.

## Squeeze Play Terminology

Before we can intelligently discuss squeeze plays, it is necessary to first learn a whole new language. This is evidenced by the words Busy, Idle, Automatic, and Positional—terms to which you have just been introduced.

# THE SIMPLE SQUEEZE IN BRIDGE

Here are a few additions to your squeeze vocabulary. You would do well to become thoroughly familiar with their meanings before continuing.

**Threat:** A card standing alone or in combination with other cards in a suit that must be defended against by an opponent. A potential winner as opposed to an actual winner. The word threat is synonymous with the word Menace.

**Single Threat:** A single card, standing alone, which represents a potential winner. The ♠ J in Illustration (A) and the ♣ Q in Illustration (C) are examples of single threats.

**Double Threat:** A card combination representing an entry card and a threat card held in the same suit. The ♣ Q 6 in Illustration (A) and the ♠ K 6 in Illustration (C) are examples of a double threat.

**Compound Threat:** A combination of cards in one suit held between declarer and dummy that contains both a length threat card and one or more entries to each hand. The length threat must be in the same hand as the squeeze card.

**Menace:** Synonymous with the word, Threat.

**Squeeze Card:** A card, usually a winner, the play of which forces a fatal discard from a Busy opponent. The Squeeze card is usually held and played by the offensive team, but it can, under unusual circumstances, be held and played by ones adversary. The ♥ K in Illustration (A) and the ♥ 8 in Illustration (C) are squeeze cards.

**The Count Down:** The playing of a series of winning tricks after the squeeze has been set. A series of winners ending with the squeeze card.

As we continue, new words and phrases will be introduced for inclusion in your Squeeze Vocabulary. Their introduction into the text will be accompanied by a footnote definition.


## The Two Suit Squeeze

The Two Suit Squeeze is another name for the Simple Squeeze or Single Squeeze. It requires finding one of your adversaries with Busy cards in two suits. If a Busy opponent exists, a squeeze may be made to operate in much the same way as a pair of pliers. The Busy hand is caught between declarer's hand and the dummy, and pressure is applied. This pressure cannot properly be brought to bear unless the squeeze card and the two threats are distributed between declarer's hand and the dummy. A Busy defender cannot be trapped by a pliers which has only one facing side.

### Rule 1

It is impossible to effect a Squeeze if both threats lie in the same hand with the Squeeze card.

In the beginning we will use only illustrations, examples and problem hands in which the squeeze card lies in the South hand. As we progress, and your squeeze skills develop, the squeeze card may be found anywhere, in the dummy, or, even in an opponent's hand.

# The BLUE Law

Before a bridge player can become an expert squeeze technician, it is first necessary to thoroughly understand the BLUE Law or BLUE formula, as it is known. This law or formula, devised by Mr. Clyde E. Love,* sets forth the four conditions which must exist in order for a squeeze to take place. Each of these conditions is represented by a letter in the key word, BLUE.

**B** One defender must have BUSY cards in two suits while his partner is helpless.

**L** Declarer must have only one more LOSER.

**U** At least one threat must lie in the UPPER Hand.

**E** There must be an ENTRY to every established threat.

### How the BLUE Law Works

Each of the letters in the key word, BLUE, stands for one of the four required squeeze conditions. Here is a detailed explanation of each of these four essential conditions as outlined in the BLUE Law.

**B** One defender must have BUSY cards in two suits while his partner is helpless.

The Busy hand, or the hand to be squeezed, must be in sole possession of controlling cards in the two squeeze suits. In Illustration (A) we have seen that defensively West holds all the controlling cards in spades and clubs, while East is helpless in these two suits. Note what happens when we interchange the ♠ J and the ♠ 9 between the South and East hands.

---

*Clyde E. Love, Professor of Mathematics, Ann Arbor, Michigan. Died 1960. A specialist on squeeze plays, whose books include *The Squeeze Play in Bridge* and *Bridge Squeezes Complete* (New York: Sterling Publishing Company, 1960).

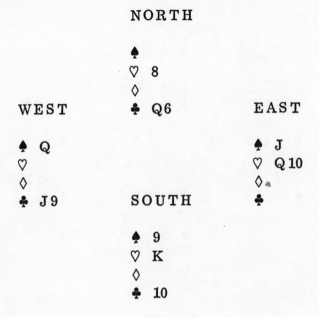

In Illustration (E) East's cards are not all valueless on defense. The ♠ J can serve as a Busy card. It defends against South's ♠ 9. The West hand is no longer made up exclusively of Busy cards. The function of the ♠ Q as a defending card against South's remaining spade can be taken over by East. The ♠ Q is now an Idle card and becomes a free discard to be played on the Squeeze trick. The squeeze fails for lack of B.

**L** Declarer must have only one more LOSER.

A simple Squeeze will not be effective unless declarer is in possession of high card winners for all but one of the remaining tricks.

In Illustration (F) condition L of the BLUE Law has not properly been met. Declarer has only two winners with four tricks remaining. As he plays his squeeze card, the ♥ 9, East is left with an extra diamond. This extra card is an Idle card and serves as a free discard. The squeeze fails for lack of L.

At some appropriate point, earlier in the play of this hand, declarer should have conceded a spade trick to West. This would have "Rectified the Count."* Without the extra Idle card in the East hand to serve as a free

NORTH

♠ 8
♡
◊ A 8 4
♣

WEST                                      EAST

♠ J 10 9                                  ♠
♡                                         ♡
◊ J                                       ◊ Q 10 9
♣                                         ♣ Q

SOUTH

♠ 5
♡ 9
◊ 6
♣ 5

discard, this squeeze would have functioned properly.

**U** At least one threat must lie in the UPPER hand.

To have the Upper hand on you at the bridge table a player must be seated to your left. He enjoys the advantage of playing after you do in just the same manner that you play after the opponent to your right. One of declarer's hands, either his own or the dummy, has the Upper hand on an intended squeeze victim. There must be at least one menace in the Upper hand.

In Illustration (A) West is the target of our squeeze. North holds the Upper hand on West. The ♣ Q 6 is the threat in the Upper hand. In illustration (B) we have transposed the East and West defensive holdings. East becomes the opponent to be squeezed. South is now the Upper hand. The ♠ J is the threat in the Upper hand.

---

*Rectify the Count: The process by which Declarer deliberately loses one or more tricks in order to correct the remaining number of losers to within one of the total number of outstanding tricks and, thereby, conform to condition L.

In Illustration (C) West is to be squeezed. Both the single menace of the ♣ Q and the double menace of the ♠ K 6 are located behind the Busy opponent. However, when the East-West hands are interchanged as they have been in Illustration (D), South becomes the Upper hand behind a Busy East. There is no threat against East in the closed hand. The squeeze fails for lack of U.

**E** There must be an ENTRY to every established threat.

Of the four conditions of the BLUE Law, E is the most perishable. It is the most vulnerable to attack, either intentionally or accidentally, by the enemy. In Illustration (F) declarer could rectify the count by leading the ♠ 5. If West wins the trick and continues the suit, East is squeezed as South ruffs the spade. However, if West is a student of squeezes, he will not play back a spade but will instead return his last diamond. This play attacks declarer's double menace before he can play his squeeze card. The squeeze fails for lack of E.

Study each of the four conditions of the BLUE Law. Review them as often as necessary until you know and understand them completely. *No simple squeeze will ever function without each of these four conditions being properly fulfilled.*

# THE FOUR ENTRY FORMS OF CONDITION E

## RULE 1

Both threats cannot lie in the same hand with the Squeeze card. Therefore, at least one threat must lie in the hand opposite the Squeeze card. If there is no entry to the hand opposite the Squeeze card, any threat held in that hand is useless.

### The First Entry Form

The hand opposite the Squeeze card contains a Double Menace.

In the First Entry Form, the second threat will always take shape as a single menace. This secondary threat may be located in the same hand with the squeeze card, or it may lie opposite the squeeze card in the same hand with the double menace.

Let's return to Illustrations (A) and (C). In (A) the ♣ Q 6 represents the double menace. It is located in the hand opposite the ♥ K, which is our squeeze card. The ♠ J is the single threat. In (C) the ♠ K 6 serves as the double threat, while the ♣ Q is the single threat. Both threats lie in the hand opposite the squeeze card, the ♥ 8.

## RULE 2

Squeeze hands involving the First Entry Form are either Automatic or Positional depending upon the location of the single menace. If the single menace is in the hand with the Squeeze card, the Squeeze is Automatic. If the single menace is in the hand opposite the Squeeze card, the hand containing the double menace, the Squeeze is Positional.

Illustrations (A) and (C) are examples of the first Entry Form. In Illustration (A) the single threat lies in the same hand as the squeeze card. The squeeze will function with equal effect if either opponent holds the Busy hand. In Illustration (C) the single threat lies in the hand opposite the squeeze card and is in the same hand with the double threat. The squeeze will operate only against a Busy West and not against a Busy East (see Illustration D). Therefore, the squeeze is Positional.

### The Second Entry Form

The hand opposite the Squeeze card contains a single menace.
Entry is provided through a compound menace, the threat card
of which lies in the same hand as the Squeeze card.

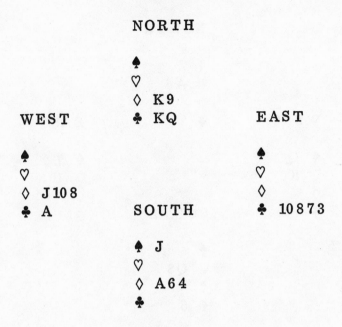

NORTH

♠
♡
◇ K9
♣ KQ

WEST        EAST

♠                      ♠
♡                      ♡
◇ J 10 8            ◇
♣ A     SOUTH     ♣ 10 8 7 3

♠ J
♡
◇ A 6 4
♣

In Illustration (G) East is the Idle hand. He can contribute nothing to the defense of the squeeze suits, diamonds and clubs. West is the Busy hand. He holds all the controlling cards in both squeeze suits. South leads the squeeze card, the ♠ J, and discards the ♣ Q from dummy. No matter what card he plays, declarer will win the balance of the tricks.

West is Squeezed.

Transpose the East-West hands for yourself. The squeeze operates with identical precision regardless of which defender holds the Busy hand. The squeeze, therefore, is Automatic.

## RULE 3

All Squeeze hands involving the Second Entry Form are Automatic and can never be Positional.

### The Third Entry Form

The hand opposite the Squeeze card contains a single menace.
The second menace consists of a Split Threat,* the Entry card
of which is in the hand opposite the Squeeze card.

*Split Threat: A split Menace. A winner and a small card opposite a threat and a small card in the same suit. See the declarer-dummy heart position in Illustration (H).

# THE SIMPLE SQUEEZE IN BRIDGE

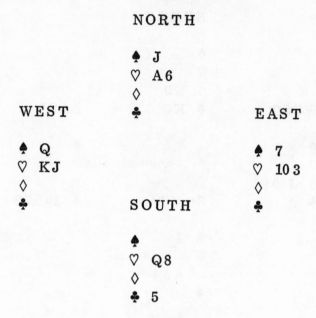

NORTH

♠ J
♡ A 6
♢
♣

WEST

♠ Q
♡ K J
♢
♣

EAST

♠ 7
♡ 10 3
♢
♣

SOUTH

♠
♡ Q 8
♢
♣ 5

In Illustration (H) we have the classic Split Threat position of Ax opposite Qx. The entry card in the Split Threat suit is the ♥ A. It and the single threat, the ♠ J, lie in the hand opposite the squeeze card, the ♠ 5. The threat card in the Split Threat position is the ♥ Q. It is the same hand with the squeeze card.

West is our intended mark. He holds Busy cards in the two squeeze suits, spades and hearts. His partner can offer no defense in either suit. South plays his squeeze card, the ♣ 5. West must either release the ♠ Q, which makes a winner of dummy's ♠ J, or he must unguard the ♥ K. Either play gives declarer the balance of the tricks.

West is Squeezed.

Notice that if the defenders' hands are interchanged, the squeeze does not operate. Dummy is squeezed before a Busy East. East discards the same suit played from dummy. In the case of a heart discard South's ♥ Q becomes a winner, but the squeeze is Positional and fails for lack of E to the South hand.

### RULE 4

All Squeezes involving the Third Entry Form are Positional. An Automatic Squeeze can never be developed using a Split Threat.

Here are two examples of complex card combinations and contain variations of a Split Threat position. In each case the entry card lies in one hand while the threat card lies in the other.

|  | AK3 |  |  | 1062 |  |
|---|---|---|---|---|---|
| QJ42 |  | 976 | 98 |  | KQJ73 |
|  | 1085 |  |  | A54 |  |

In example (a), the threat card is the ♠ 10 in the South hand, while the entries lie in the North hand. Example (b) Illustrates an entry in the South hand ( ♠ A) and a threat card, (the ♣ 10) in the North hand.

### The Fourth Entry Form
>Two Blocked Threats
>Facing Each Other

This entry form enjoys the somewhat exotic name of the Criss-Cross Squeeze. It is a rare situation that will not make up one per cent of all the squeeze situations you will face. Until we take it up later in this text (see Chapter V) it is only necessary that you be aware of its existence.

### Complete Deals

All fifty-two card deals shown in this text are divided into two categories, Examples and Problem Hands. Examples are used to instruct. They will appear in double dummy form with all four hands exposed. Problem hands are meant to test the reader on what he has already learned. They will first be shown with only the reader's hand and dummy exposed. You will have an opportunity to determine your own line of play before the complete deal is displayed.

These illustrations are not just isolated card combinations contrived to demonstrate the various squeeze endings. Each variation illustrates an end position from an actual deal. Now you will encounter the complete deals from which these earlier Illustrations evolved. Study each lay-out carefully and see if you can declare the hand so as to arrive at the proper end position for a squeeze.

NORTH

♠ 5
♡ 8 3
◇ A K Q J 10 6
♣ K Q 6 3

WEST

♠ K Q 10 4
♡ J 7 2
◇ 4
♣ J 9 8 7 2

EAST

♠ 9 8 7 3 2
♡ Q 10 9 5 4
◇ 7 3
♣ 4

SOUTH

♠ A J 6
♡ A K 6
◇ 9 8 5 2
♣ A 10 5

The Auction:

| NORTH | EAST | SOUTH | WEST |
|-------|------|-------|------|
| 1 ◇ | Pass | 3 N.T. | Pass |
| 4 ♣ | Pass | 4 ◇ | Pass |
| 4 N.T. | Pass | 5 ♠ | Pass |
| 5 N.T. | Pass | 6 ◇ | Pass |
| 7 N.T. | Pass | Pass | Pass |

Opening Lead: ♠ K

North can be sure of twelve winners following the Blackwood sequence. He bids a grand slam at No Trump hoping to find the ♣ J or some other plus value in the South hand.

Declarer wins the opening lead in the closed hand and considers his prospects. The hand would seem to depend on developing four tricks in the club suit. If the suit divides evenly, or, if the ♣ J is singleton or doubleton in either opponent's hand, we have our thirteenth trick. A small club is played to dummy's ♣ K and a club is returned to South's ♣ A. East fails to follow suit to the second round of the suit. It is time to check out the BLUE Law for a squeeze against West.

## Condition B

West is known to hold the balance of the club suit, and unless he has made a very unusual opening lead, he also has the ♥ Q. This leaves him Busy protecting both black suits, since East is known not to have any clubs and cannot defend against South's ♠ J. Condition B is met.

## Condition L

There are twelve winners between the North-South hands: the ♠ A, two hearts, six diamonds, and three top clubs. This satisfies Condition L.

## Condition U

What are our threats? The ♠ J held by South is a single threat and dummy's ♣ Q6 is a double threat. North holds the Upper hand on West. The double threat in clubs satisfies Condition U.

## Condition E

Do we have entries to our threats? If we cash all of the diamonds in dummy and then return to the closed hand with a heart, we can use the second high heart as our squeeze card. We are in the same hand with our single threat, the ♠ J, and the ♣ 10 provides access to the ♣ Q 6 in the North hand. This fulfills Condition E as the First Entry Form. With the single threat of the ♠ J in the same hand with our squeeze card, the ♥ K, our squeeze is of the Automatic variety and would function against either opponent even though our squeeze victim is known to be West.

With each of the four conditions of the BLUE Law satisfied, it is time to operate our Squeeze. Begin the count down by playing all six of dummy's diamond winners. The ♠ 6 and the ♥ 6 are discarded from the South hand. The play of a heart to the ace in the closed hand brings about this three-card end position.

NORTH

♠  
♡ 8  
◊  
♣ Q6

WEST            EAST

♠ Q                ♠ 9  
♡                   ♡ Q 10  
◊                   ◊  
♣ J9      SOUTH      ♣

♠ J  
♡ K  
◊  
♣ 10

And here we have the same position as that shown in Illustration (A). As the squeeze card, the ♥ K, is played, West is squeezed.

```
                        NORTH

                      ♠ AK63
                      ♡ Q96
                      ◇ Q63
        WEST          ♣ QJ6          EAST

    ♠ QJ1087                     ♠ 94
    ♡ 752                        ♡ 4
    ◇ J4                         ◇ 10975
    ♣ AK3         SOUTH          ♣ 987542

                      ♠ 52
                      ♡ AKJ1083
                      ◇ AK82
                      ♣ 10
```

## The Auction:

| SOUTH | WEST | NORTH | EAST |
|-------|------|-------|------|
| 1 ♡ | 1 ♠ | 3 N.T. | Pass |
| 4 ◇ | Pass | 4 ♡ | Pass |
| 4 N.T. | Pass | 5 ◇ | Pass |
| 6 ♡ | Pass | Pass | Pass |

Opening Lead: ♣ K

North-South reach a small slam in hearts that shows excellent prospects of making. West leads the ♣ K. He is pessin.istic about his chances of being able to cash the    A and rightly so. He shifts to the ♠ Q.

Declarer wins the spade in dummy and extracts the opponents' trump in three rounds. If they had been divided two-two, the fourth diamond could have been ruffed in dummy. The diamond suit is tried next. When it fails to divide three-three, it is time to apply the old addage, "when all else fails, squeeze."

## Condition B

West's overcall marks him with a five-card spade suit. His opening lead indicates he also holds the ♣ A. This leaves East Idle in both black suits and satisfies condition B.

## Condition L

The defense has won one trick. We have eleven winners of the twelve tricks remaining: two spades, six hearts, and three diamonds. Condition L is met.

## Condition U

It is time to check out our threats. The ♣ Q is a single threat against West's ♣ A. The ♠ K 6 will serve as our double threat against West's known spade length. Both threats lie in the Upper hand behind West. Please note that if East were our intended mark, the Squeeze would fail for lack of U.

## Condition E

The First Entry Form (Positional) is present. Both the single menace of the ♣ Q and the double menace of the ♠ K 6 lie in the hand opposite the squeeze card. The ♠ 5 provides the needed entry.

It is time to operate the squeeze machine. Declarer plays all of his remaining trumps but one, which brings about this end position.

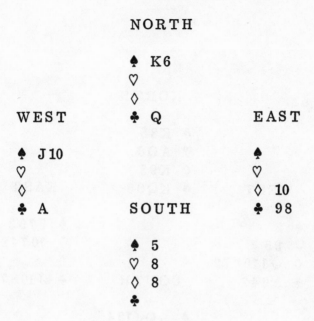

NORTH

♠ K6
♡
◇
♣ Q

WEST

♠ J 10
♡
◇
♣ A

EAST

♠
♡
◇ 10
♣ 9 8

SOUTH

♠ 5
♡ 8
◇ 8
♣

And this is the same Squeeze position shown in Illustration (C).

Most neophyte bridge players look upon their last piece of trump as some sort of security blanket. They grip this last master card like grim death in the belief that as long as they have it nothing bad can happen to them. On the contrary. This is not so. Until such time as you are willing to face the realization that the last trump is no more valuable than any other winner in your hand, and that there is no special point bonus for taking the last trick, you will never be able to execute a squeeze. PLAY YOUR LAST TRUMP!!! It squeezes West.

```
                      NORTH

                   ♠ K85
                   ♡ AQ6
                   ◇ K95
       WEST        ♣ KQ95        EAST

     ♠ 2                        ♠ 9763
     ♡ 95                       ♡ 10742
     ◇ QJ10872                  ◇
     ♣ A642        SOUTH        ♣ J10873

                   ♠ AQJ104
                   ♡ KJ83
                   ◇ A643
                   ♣
```

The Auction:

| NORTH  | EAST | SOUTH | WEST |
|--------|------|-------|------|
| 1 N.T. | Pass | 2 ♣   | Pass |
| 2 ◇    | Pass | 3 ♠   | Pass |
| 4 ♠    | Pass | 6 ♠   | Pass |
| Pass   | Pass |       |      |

Opening Lead: ◇ Q

West opens the ♦ Q. North plays low and East trumps. He returns the ♣ J. Declarer ruffs and plays two rounds of trump. If the outstanding trump had fallen, he would be able to trump the last diamond in dummy. It is time to look for a squeeze.

## Condition B

West is known to be Busy in diamonds. He should also have the ♣ A. Condition B is met.

## Condition L

The defense has taken one trick. South can count eleven winners with twelve tricks remaining: five spades, four hearts, and two diamonds. This satisfies Condition L.

## Condition U

West is our candidate for this squeeze. Either the ♣ K or ♣ Q will do nicely as a single threat in the Upper hand. Condition U is in order.

## Condition E

The Second Entry Form is present. Our single menace in clubs lies in the hand opposite the squeeze card, the ♠ J. A compound menace in diamonds provides the necessary entry to the single menace and back again, depending on what discarding decision the Busy opponent to our left makes.

It is time to put our squeeze into operation. We begin by taking East's last trump away from him. The count down consists of running our four heart winners, which brings about this end position.

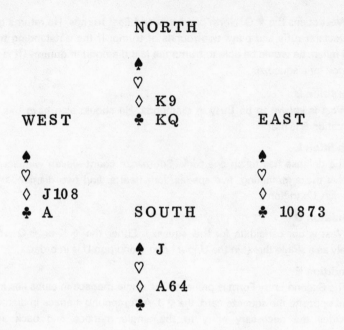

NORTH

♠
♡
◊ K9
♣ KQ

WEST

♠
♡
◊ J 10 8
♣ A

EAST

♠
♡
◊
♣ 10 8 7 3

SOUTH

♠ J
♡
◊ A 6 4
♣

This is the same end position as that shown in Illustration (G). South's play of the ♠ J Squeezes West.

Take note that this squeeze would have been equally effective if East had held the Busy cards in diamonds and clubs. It is, as are all squeezes involving the Second Entry Form, an Automatic Squeeze.

# THE SIMPLE SQUEEZE IN BRIDGE

Declarer wins Trick 1 in Dummy with the ♠A and stops to survey the situation. He can count only twelve winners and has no prospects for a thirteenth. Time to check out the BLUE Law.

## Condition B

There are only twelve high card points that we can't account for. West must have virtually all of them for his opening bid. This leaves him Busy in spades and hearts.

## Condition L

We can count twelve winners: two major suit aces, two diamonds, and eight clubs.

## Condition U

We need a threat in the Upper hand. The ♥Q lies with South and will not satisfy U if we are out to squeeze West. The ♠J in the North hand, however, is made to order for our purposes.

## Condition E

This is the Third Entry Form. The split threat in hearts provides the needed entry to the ♠J. Our single threat is properly positioned opposite our squeeze card. What is our squeeze card? The last club.

Declarer sets up his squeeze by pulling two rounds of trump with the ♣K Q. Next he cashes his ♦A and then enters the open hand with the ♣A. The ♦K is played and the remaining spade is pitched from the closed hand. The ♠8 is trumped and the count down begins. South plays all of his clubs but one to bring about this squeeze ending. It is the same as that shown in Illustration (H).

### NORTH

♠ AJ8
♡ A652
◇ K63
♣ A104

| WEST | | EAST |
|------|--|------|
| ♠ KQ1094 | | ♠ 752 |
| ♡ KJ974 | | ♡ 103 |
| ◇ QJ10 | | ◇ 987542 |
| ♣ QJ10 | | ♣ J7 |

### SOUTH

♠ 63
♡ Q8
◇ A
♣ KQ986532

## The Auction:

| WEST | NORTH | EAST | SOUTH |
|------|-------|------|-------|
| 1 ♠ | 1 N.T. | Pass | 3 ♣ |
| Pass | 3 N.T. | Pass | 4 N.T. |
| Pass | 5 ♠ | Pass | 5 N.T. |
| Pass | 6 ◇ | Pass | 7 ♣ |
| Pass | Pass | Pass | |

## Opening Lead: ♠ K

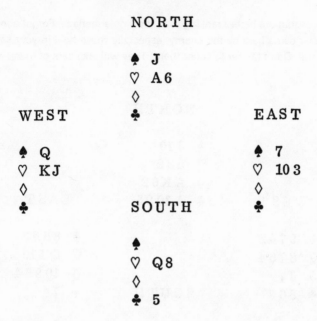

NORTH

♠ J
♡ A 6
◇
♣

WEST                    EAST

♠ Q                    ♠ 7
♡ K J                  ♡ 10 3
◇                      ◇
♣                      ♣

SOUTH

♠
♡ Q 8
◇
♣ 5

South plays his squeeze card, the ♣ 5. West is squeezed. North, the Upper hand, discards to the squeeze trick after West. If the East-West hands had been reversed, North would be forced to discard to the squeeze trick before a Busy East. In the case of a heart discard, South's ♥ Q becomes a winner when a Busy East discards the ♥ J, but there is no entry to the South hand to cash it. The squeeze fails for lack of E. All Third Entry Form Squeezes are Positional.

### Counting Out the Squeeze

In examples (1) through (4) you knew which opponent you were squeezing and exactly what cards he held. This may not always be the case. After gaining a little experience, you will find yourself playing for squeezes that may or may not exist and where you are not sure which of your opponents is the Busy opponent.

When playing out a squeeze position, it is not necessary to keep track of every card played by both opponents. Counting is not only time consuming and tiresome, it can also prove to be confusing. Above all it is unnecessary. Once the BLUE conditions have been recognized and the squeeze is set, declarer should occupy himself with only one concern. He must watch for those cards that are higher ranking than the single menace. Forget about all of the other cards held by the enemy, especially those held in your second menace suit. Don't bother to count them! They will take care of themselves.

### NORTH

♠ J 10
♡ 5 3 2
◊ A K 6 2
♣ A 10 9 5

### WEST

♠ 9 7 4 2
♡ 8 7 6 4
◊ J 7
♣ 8 6 3

### EAST

♠ 8 6 5 3
♡ Q J 10
◊ 10 9 5 4
♣ 7 4

### SOUTH

♠ A K Q
♡ A K 9
◊ Q 8 3
♣ K Q J 2

## The Auction:

| NORTH | EAST | SOUTH | WEST |
|-------|------|-------|------|
| 1 ◊ | Pass | 4 N.T. | Pass |
| 5 ♡ | Pass | 5 N.T. | Pass |
| 6 ◊ | Pass | 7 N.T. | Pass |
| Pass | Pass | | |

## Opening Lead: ♡ 8

After using Blackwood, South can count twelve tricks. He bids 7 NT hoping for some small additional value in the North hand that would make his grand slam a virtual lay-down.

West opens the ♥ 8 upon which East plays the ♥ Q. Our contract would seem to hinge upon a three-three division of the diamond suit. Is there any other possibility to fall back on? Check out the BLUE Law for a possible squeeze.

## Condition B

For the moment, let's assume the diamond suit does not divide evenly. What pressure can be applied to a defender who holds diamond length? Despite East's obvious false-card to Trick 1, the opening lead suggests that the ♥ Q J 10 lie with East. If one defender can be found with four or more diamonds plus either the ♥ Q J 10 or any heart holding that is five or more cards in length, Condition B is met.

## The Process of Assumption

Take special notice of the Process of Assumption as outlined in Condition B. It is rare indeed that Declarer is provided with perfect insight as to his opponent's exact holdings. Therefore, Condition B must often be assumed to exist and the hand then played accordingly. If the cards lie favorably, as we hope or assume, the squeeze will work; if not, little had been lost.

## Condition L

South was sure of twelve tricks before he ever saw the dummy. This situation has not changed. Condition L is satisfied.

## Condition U

It is time to check out our threats. If the top hearts are cashed, the ♥ 9 becomes a single menace. The ♦ A and ♦ Q can also be played leaving a double menace of ♦ K 6 in dummy. The ♥ 9 satisfies Condition U if East is to be our victim. The double menace in diamonds held by Dummy fulfills Condition U on the off chance that West is our man.

## Condition E

Next check for entries. The double threat of the ♦ K 6 lies in the hand opposite the squeeze card. A small diamond provides access. This satisfies the First Entry Form. The single menace of the ♥ 9 is held in the closed hand with the squeeze card. Our squeeze is Automatic. What is our squeeze card? Actually we have a choice. Let's make it the ♠ Q.

With all four conditions of the BLUE Law met, it is time to operate our squeeze. Win the opening lead with the ♥ A and cash the ♥ K. East's play of the ♥ J is duly noted. Next you can play the ♦ A and ♦ Q to create a classic double menace. Now start the count down. Run your four club winners followed by the ♠ A K. Here is the end position.

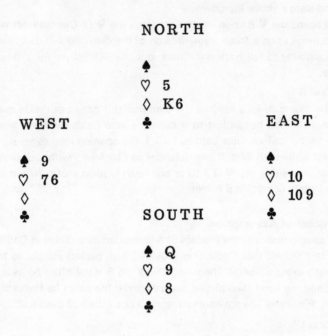

NORTH

♠
♡ 5
◊ K6
♣

WEST

♠ 9
♡ 76
◊
♣

EAST

♠
♡ 10
◊ 10 9
♣

SOUTH

♠ Q
♡ 9
◊ 8
♣

At the time Declarer checked out the four conditions of BLUE, he should have realized that his ♥ 9 would eventually become the single threat in his hoped for squeeze.

## RULE 5

Count only the single menace suit. The second Squeeze suit will count itself.

Can you see why it is so important to watch only the single menace suit? You have played this entire hand out on the assumption that the Busy cards in the red suits are in the East hand. What if, in fact, the opponents' hands are distributed like this?

|  WEST  |  EAST  |
| --- | --- |
| ♠ 74 | ♠ 986532 |
| ♡ 108764 | ♡ QJ |
| ◊ J754 | ◊ 109 |
| ♣ 86 | ♣ 743 |

Avoid confusing yourself with too much card counting. This is an Automatic Single Squeeze. It will operate with equal effect against either adversary, if he happens to hold Busy cards in both squeeze suits. If your single threat, the ♥ 9, is not a winner after the squeeze card has been played, lead your diamond to dummy. If the squeeze did not work, the diamonds may have been divided three-three all the time, in which case, even those players without your newly acquired knowledge will make the contract.

THE SIMPLE SQUEEZE IN BRIDGE

NORTH

♠ KJ5
♡ 852
♦ 1094
♣ AK93

WEST

♠ 6
♡ AK3
♦ QJ762
♣ QJ72

EAST

♠ 8742
♡ Q974
♦ 853
♣ 105

SOUTH

♠ AQ1093
♡ J106
♦ AK
♣ 864

The Auction:

| SOUTH | WEST | NORTH | EAST |
|-------|------|-------|------|
| 1 ♠ | Dbl. | Redbl. | Pass |
| Pass | 2 ◊ | Pass | Pass |
| 2 ♠ | Pass | 4 ♠ | Pass |
| Pass | Pass | | |

Opening Lead: ♡ K

30

North-South bid their way to an ambitious game in spades that would seem to have no chance at all of making. West wins the first two tricks with the ♥ A K, and, seeing his partner's high-card signal, continues the suit. East takes his ♥ Q and shifts to the ♦ 8. Declarer wins the ♦ A and stops to survey the situation. He cannot afford to lose any more tricks if he is to make this contract. Yet, he does not have enough winners to take the balance of the tricks. Time to check out the BLUE Law.

## Condition B

As we pointed out before, we are forced to make assumptions about our opponents' hands if our squeeze is to work. From East's play of the ♦ 8 we suspect West owns the ♦ Q J. If he is also in sole control of clubs by holding four or more cards in the suit, or specifically the ♣ Q J 10, he can be squeezed.

## Condition L

The defense has won the first three tricks. We have high card winners for nine of the ten tricks remaining: five spades, two diamonds, and two clubs. Condition L is satisfied.

## Condition U

Clubs and diamonds are our squeeze suits. The ♦ 10 is the single threat, while the dummy's club holding serves as our double threat. Both threats lie in the Upper hand on West. Please note that should East by some chance control both clubs and diamonds, the squeeze will fail for lack of U. The South hand holds the Upper hand on East, but contains no threat. The East-West hands are not interchangeable; therefore, the squeeze is Positional.

## Condition E

The First Entry Form (Positional) is present. North has a single menace, the ♦ 10, which is easily recognizable once South plays the ♦ K. Clubs are the double menace and provide the necessary entry to the North hand.

It is now time to operate the squeeze machine. Trumps are drawn in four rounds. Declarer plays a club to the Ace and a diamond back to the king in the closed hand. This will bring about the classic end position shown below.

### NORTH

♠
♡
◇ 10
♣ K9

### WEST          EAST

♠              ♠
♡              ♡ 9
◇ Q            ◇ 5
♣ QJ    **SOUTH**    ♣ 10

♠ 10
♡
◇
♣ 86

South leads his last trump, the ♠10, which squeezes West Positionally.

NORTH

♠ Q10
♡ Q84
◇ A2
♣ Q86532

WEST

♠ 8732
♡ 97
◇ Q9853
♣ J10

EAST

♠ J5
♡ J1063
◇ J107
♣ K974

SOUTH

♠ AK964
♡ AK52
◇ K64
♣ A

## The Auction:

| SOUTH | WEST | NORTH | EAST |
|---|---|---|---|
| 1 ♠ | Pass | 1 N.T. | Pass |
| 3 ♡ | Pass | 3 ♠ | Pass |
| 4 ◇ | Pass | 4 ♡ | Pass |
| 4 ♠ | Pass | 4 N.T. | Pass |
| 5 ♠ | Pass | 6 ♠ | Pass |
| Pass | Pass | | |

## Opening Lead: ♣ J

A fine small slam is reached on a delicate auction. The first nine tricks are played in a straightforward manner. The ♣ J opening lead is won with the ♣ A followed by two high diamonds and a diamond ruff in Dummy. The ♠ Q, a high heart to the closed hand, and three more trumps follow. The remaining cards are these.

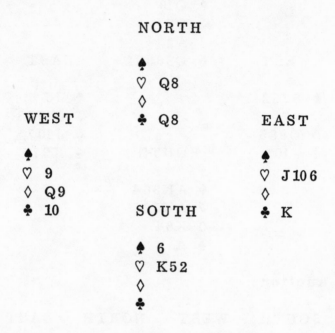

NORTH

♠
♡ Q8
◇
♣ Q8

WEST

♠
♡ 9
◇ Q9
♣ 10

EAST

♠
♡ J 10 6
◇
♣ K

SOUTH

♠ 6
♡ K52
◇
♣

At this point the contract is assured, but the game is match-points. An overtrick is of vital importance to the score, particularly if it can be made by other than some mundane set of circumstances such as finding the heart suit splitting three-three.

If the heart suit does not divide evenly, can anything be done about it? Go to the BLUE Law for a possible squeeze.

If the heart suit divides evenly, or if the clubs and hearts are guarded by separate defenders, we will receive the same score as anyone else who bids this slam. However, if a single defender started with four or more hearts and the ♣ K, **Condition B** is satisfied and a squeeze is possible. Again we are working on an assumption, but what do we have to lose? If the hoped for combination of cards exist, we will gain a trick that would not normally be ours for a very fine match-point result.

**Condition L** is met. We have two heart tricks and a spade winner out of the remaining four tricks.

**Condition U** is in order. There is one threat in each hand, the ♣ Q in dummy, and the long heart in declarer's hand. There is a threat in the Upper hand should either opponent hold Busy cards in both threat suits.

**Condition E** is also satisfied. The Second Entry Form is present. The ♣ Q is an obvious single menace against the defender holding the ♣ K. It lies, as it should, in the hand opposite the squeeze card, the ♠ 6. A compound menace in hearts provides the necessary entry to the single menace and back again to the long suit threat.

It is now time to put our squeeze into operation. Our count down consists of only one trick, the squeeze trick. The play of the ♠ 6, our squeeze card, activates our squeeze as the ♣ 8 is thrown from the open hand. We need only watch for one card, the ♣ K. If it does not appear, we play our remaining hearts.

Take note that this squeeze is equally effective against either defender. It is, as are all squeezes involving the Second Entry Form, an Automatic Squeeze. The Busy hand could have been West, in which case the squeeze would have operated with equal efficiency.

```
                        NORTH

                     ♠ A963
                     ♡ AQJ
                     ◊ J62
        WEST         ♣ K109          EAST

     ♠ K8                          ♠ J1072
     ♡ 87                          ♡ 63
     ◊ AKQ                         ◊ 10974
     ♣ QJ8643        SOUTH         ♣ 752

                     ♠ ♠ Q54
                     ♡ K109542
                     ◊ 853
                     ♣ A
```

The Auction:

| WEST | NORTH | EAST | SOUTH |
|------|-------|------|-------|
| 1 ♣  | Dbl.  | Pass | 4 ♡   |
| Pass | Pass  | Pass |       |

Opening Lead: ◊ K

South moves directly to game in hearts in response to his partner's take-out double. West takes the first three diamond tricks for the defense and exits from his hand by leading a trump. Declarer wins Trick 4 with the ♥ A and goes to work on the four conditions of the BLUE Law.

**Condition B.** West is known to hold the majority of the outstanding high cards by virtue of his opening bid. If his values include the ♠ K plus the ♣ Q J or a seven-card club suit, he is Busy in the black suits while East is Idle.

**Condition L** is in good order. Declarer lost the first three tricks. Of the ten tricks remaining he has nine winners: a spade, six hearts, and two clubs.

**Condition U** requires a threat in the Upper hand. The ♠ Q lies with South and will not satisfy U if we are out to Squeeze West. The ♣10 in the North hand, however, is part of a blocked threat. If the ♣ A K are cashed, the ♣10 becomes a single threat in the Upper hand against West.

**Condition E** exists as the Third Entry Form. The split threat in spades provides the needed entry to the ♣ 10. Our single threat is properly positioned opposite the ♥10, which is the squeeze card.

Declarer sets up his squeeze by clearing the ♣A, returning to dummy in trump, and cashing the ♣ K. The ♣10 now is established as the single menace. The closed hand is re-entered by overtaking dummy's last trump honor. The count down consists of running trumps, arriving at the following end position.

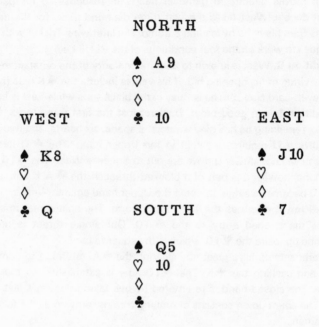

**NORTH**

♠ A 9
♡
◇
♣ 10

**WEST**

♠ K 8
♡
◇
♣ Q

**EAST**

♠ J 10
♡
◇
♣ 7

**SOUTH**

♠ Q 5
♡ 10
◇
♣

Declarer activates the squeeze machine by leading his last trump, the ♥ 10. According to Rule 5, the only cards to watch for are those higher than the single menace. In this case they are the ♣ Q J. If the opposition has not parted with both of these cards by the time West follows to the squeeze trick, the ♣ 10 is not a winner and must be discarded.

North has the Upper hand against West and discards to the squeeze trick after him. If East had been the Busy hand, North would be forced to discard first and our Squeeze would fail for lack of E. Spade discards by North and a Busy East would establish the ♠ Q as a winner, but there is no entry to the South hand to cash it.

### How to Rectify the Count

Not every squeeze hand is dealt in a ready to go pattern. It is sometimes necessary for declarer to make a minor adjustment or two prior to running the count down and applying the squeeze.

### NORTH

♠ 863
♡ AQ52
◊ A843
♣ A8

WEST                                          EAST

♠ QJ10974                                     ♠ 2
♡ K84                                         ♡ 73
◊ J7                                          ◊ Q10952
♣ 107                                         ♣ QJ963

### SOUTH

♠ AK5
♡ J1096
◊ K6
♣ K542

## The Auction:

| WEST | NORTH | EAST | SOUTH |
|------|-------|------|-------|
| 2 ♠* | Dbl. | Pass | 4 N.T. |
| Pass | 5 ♠ | Pass | 6 ♡ |
| Pass | Pass | Pass | |

* Weak 2 Bid

Opening Lead: ♠ Q

North-South stretch their values and bid a slam on this hand. Declarer wins the ♠ A and takes the heart finesse, playing three rounds of the suit. If West shows up with only two trumps, the contract can be made by leaving the last trump outstanding. A spade play from Dummy can be trumped by East or not. Declarer can then scramble for twelve tricks on a cross ruff. When West is found to hold three trumps, South must check out the BLUE Law and look for a squeeze.

**Condition B** cannot be developed against West. If his weak two bid is to be believed, he holds a six-card spade suit plus the three hearts we have already seen. Without the possibility of a second suit he is not a candidate for a squeeze. On the other hand this leaves East with ten minor suit cards. We nominate him as our squeeze victim.

If East holds five cards in each minor, West is unable to protect either one. This is a logical assumption, when you consider that West did not lead a minor suit singleton in an attempt to gain a ruff.

**Condition L** is considered next. Count the winners: two spades, two diamonds, two clubs, and five hearts by virtue of a club ruff in dummy. This total of eleven winners is within one trick of making our contract, but it is two tricks away from winning the balance of the tricks. Our squeeze is about to fail for lack of L. What can be done about it? Simple; lose a trick. But where? How about spades?

Declarer's best course of action is to immediately give up trick five to West by ducking a spade into his hand. This will rectify the count and bring Condition L back into line.

**Condition U** requires a threat in the Upper hand. South holds the Upper hand on East. After cashing two top clubs, Declarer ruffs one in dummy. His remaining card in the suit, the ♣ 5, becomes a single menace against East.

**Condition E** is present in the First Entry Form (Automatic). Dummy contains a double menace in diamonds. South is left with the ♣ 5 as a single menace plus the ♥ 9, his squeeze card.

Let's go over the play again. Declarer wins the opening spade lead and takes the heart finesse, drawing trumps in three rounds. He next passes a spade to West to rectify the count. West is most likely to return a spade for fear of finessing his partner with any other play. Clubs come next with the third round being ruffed in dummy. The closed hand is reentered by way of the ♦ K to arrive at this end position.

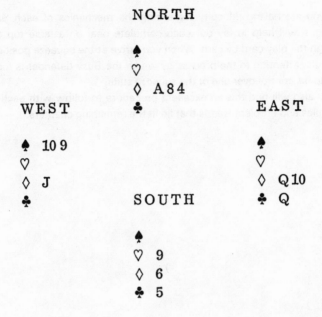

NORTH

♠
♡
♢ A 8 4
♣

WEST                                    EAST

♠ 10 9                                  ♠
♡                                       ♡
♢ J                                     ♢ Q 10
♣              SOUTH                     ♣ Q

♠
♡ 9
♢ 6
♣ 5

This is the same Squeeze ending as that shown in Illustration (F), but the count has now been rectified. Declarer squeezes East by leading his last Trump, the ♥ 9. Early in the play of this hand, as declarer went about the business of constructing his squeeze, he should have visualized an ending where the ♣ 5 would be his single threat. Therefore, this is the only suit he must count. It is not even necessary to know which clubs are outstanding. It is only important to know if there are any. It is safe to assume that if there is a club outstanding, it will beat the ♣ 5. Take a moment. Return to Illustration (F). You will see how important it was to duck the spade to West early in the hand. Without this play we would have a squeeze as pictured in (F) that fails for lack of L.

## SUMMARY, CHAPTER I

This completes our fundamental discussion of the BLUE Law. The four required conditions and the first three entry forms represent the foundation stones upon which this entire text will be based. If your mind harbors the slightest doubt that you are thoroughly and completely conversant with the material covered thus far, invest the time needed to re-read this entire chapter before continuing.

# THE SIMPLE SQUEEZE IN BRIDGE

If you are having difficulty visualizing the mechanics of each Squeeze ending, it will help to lay out each complete deal on a table top and go through the play card by card. When you arrive at the squeeze position, pay particular attention to the process by which the Busy defender is forced to give up his control over one of the squeeze suits.

You also will find this an excellent procedure to follow with each of the Examples and Problem Hands that lie in the remaining chapters.

Chapter II

# Elementary Squeeze Problems

You now have a basic understanding of the fundamentals of squeeze technique. It is time to improve your abilities through practice. Each Problem Hand is a mini-test. To begin with you will be given only the North-South cards. The same information you would have under normal playing conditions is supplied. Study both hands, the auction, the opening lead, and the play to the first trick or tricks as shown. The end position needed to effect the squeeze is unknown. Apply your knowledge of the BLUE Law to each deal. Picture the opposing hands as you hope to find them and plan your play accordingly.

After you think you have solved the problem, consult the complete lay-out of all four hands which is displayed next. A complete explanation of how the hand should be played and the reasoning behind the play is given. The actual squeeze ending is also shown.

Keep a 3 x 5 file card or other suitable bookmark handy so you may cover up the complete deal while you make up your mind as to how you wish to play each problem hand.

NORTH    The Auction:

♠ AQJ       EAST    SOUTH    WEST    NORTH
♡ AQ52
◊ Q83       1 ◊     Pass     Pass    Dbl.
♣ AKJ       Pass    1 ♡      Pass    2 ◊
            Dbl.    3 ♡      Pass    4 ♡
            Pass    Pass     Pass

   SOUTH
            Opening Lead: ◊ J
♠ 106
♡ KJ9863    Trick 1: ◊J-Q-K-4
◊ 1064      Trick 2: ◊A-6-5-3
♣ 32        Trick 3: ◊9-10-8 West ♡7
            Trick 4: ♠8 ?

Plan your play.

NORTH

♠ A Q J
♡ A Q 5 2
◊ Q 8 3
♣ A K J

WEST

♠ 8 7 4 3 2
♡ 10 7
◊ J 5
♣ 10 7 6 4

EAST

♠ K 9 5
♡ 4
◊ A K 9 7 2
♣ Q 9 8 5

SOUTH

♠ 10 6
♡ K J 9 8 6 3
◊ 10 6 4
♣ 3 2

North showed poor judgment by placing his partner in a heart game. There would have been no problem had he made himself declarer at 3 NT, leaving the strong hand, East, on lead.

At hearts, West leads his partner's bid suit. East wins two diamonds and returns the ♦ 9 for West to trump. Reading the high diamond return as a request for spades, West plays the ♠8.

It's time for declarer to take stock of the situation. To finesse the spade would be an exercise in futility. East's hand reads out like an open book. In addition to the ♦ K he must hold both the ♠ K and the ♣ Q for his opening bid. Can East be squeezed? Let's go over the four conditions of the BLUE Law.

**Condition B.** East should have the two missing black honor cards and is, therefore, Busy in two suits.

**Condition L.** Declarer has lost three tricks. Of the ten remaining tricks he can win nine: six hearts, two clubs, and the ♠ A.

**Condition U.** South has the Upper hand on East. The ♠ 10 is equal in value to the ♠ Q J in Dummy. It can serve as the single threat against the ♠ K, allowing North's ♠ Q J to serve as free discards.

45

# THE SIMPLE SQUEEZE IN BRIDGE

**Condition E.** The First Entry Form (Automatic) exists. Dummy has a double threat in clubs while South holds the ♠10 as a single threat plus the squeeze card. What is the squeeze card? Declarer's last trump.

To set the squeeze you have only to win the ♠A and run the heart suit. This is the squeeze position as the last trump is led.

NORTH

♠ Q
♡
♢
♣ AKJ

WEST

♠ 7
♡
♢
♣ 10 76

EAST

♠ K
♡
♢
♣ Q98

SOUTH

♠ 10
♡ 3
♢
♣ 32

NORTH        The Auction:

♠ J9652      NORTH   EAST   SOUTH   WEST
♡ Q6
◇ K83        Pass    Pass   1 ♡     Dbl.
♣ 653        1 ♠     2 ♣    3 ◇     Pass
             3 ♡     Pass   4 ♡     Pass
             Pass    Pass

SOUTH

             Opening Lead: ♠ K
♠ 84
♡ AKJ10 9 3  Trick 1: ♠K-2-3-4
◇ AQ62       Trick 2: ♠7-5-Q-8
♣ K          Trick 3: ♣Q-K-A-3
             Trick 4: ♣9 ?

Plan your play.

### NORTH

♠ J9652
♡ Q6
◇ K83
♣ 653

### WEST

♠ AK107
♡ 72
◇ J1075
♣ A98

### EAST

♠ Q3
♡ 854
◇ 94
♣ QJ10742

### SOUTH

♠ 84
♡ AKJ1093
◇ AQ62
♣ K

West's opening lead holds the first trick as RHO plays the ♦ 3. East's failure to start a high-low places him with a singleton or the ♦ Q. West underleads spades hoping his partner can ruff and return a club to beat the contract. East wins with one black queen and returns the other.

South trumps West's ♣ 9 in the closed hand and considers how to proceed. Squeeze endings should be given consideration at all times, but not to the exclusion of perfectly normal lines of play. Declarer should play two rounds of trump ending in dummy. He ruffs a spade in hopes the suit will divide evenly. Only when this fails is a squeeze considered.

**Condition B.** West is known to own the ♠ K. If he also holds four or more diamonds he has Busy cards in two suits. This gives declarer something more than just a three-three split in the diamond suit to fall back on.

**Condition L.** Only if diamonds fail to divide three-three does condition L exist.

**Condition U.** North holds the Upper hand on West. The ♠ J fulfills condition U.

**Condition E.** The Second Entry Form is present. The ♠ J is a single menace in the Upper hand. The diamond suit is a compound menace and supplies the entry needed to the Upper hand. The diamond length is in the South hand with the squeeze card, as it should be. What is our squeeze card? The last trump. All but one of the remaining hearts in the closed hand are cashed leaving this squeeze ending.

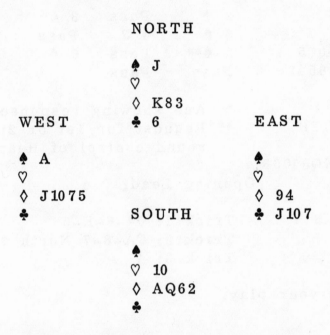

NORTH

♠ J
♡
◇ K 8 3
♣ 6

WEST

♠ A
♡
◇ J 10 7 5
♣

EAST

♠
♡
◇ 9 4
♣ J 10 7

SOUTH

♠
♡ 10
◇ A Q 6 2
♣

Declarer plays his ♥ 10 and discards a small diamond or the last club from dummy. There is no need to count a single card. If the ♠ A has not appeared, the diamonds are run just as if they had been evenly divided all the time. As the cards lie, LHO is caught in a spade-diamond squeeze.

## The Auction:

| NORTH | SOUTH | WEST | NORTH | EAST |
|-------|-------|------|-------|------|
| ♠ 85 | 2 ♠ | Pass | 3 ◊* | 3 ♡ |
| ♡ 6 | 3 ♠ | 4 ♡ | Pass | Pass |
| ◊ A 10 6 5 | 5 ♠** | Pass | 6 ♠ | Pass |
| ♣ 986542 | Pass | Pass | | |

           *   Ace showing response.

SOUTH      ** Request for 1st or 2nd
                     round control of Hearts.

♠ AKQJ10 6 3

♡ 85       Opening Lead: ♡ 4

◊ K

♣ AK3        Trick 1: ♡4-6-K-5
                Trick 2: ♡A-8-7 North ♠5
                Trick 3: ?

Plan your play.

### NORTH

♠ 85
♡ 6
◊ A 10 6 5
♣ 9 8 6 5 4 2

**WEST**

♠
♡ Q 10 7 4
◊ Q J 8 7 4 2
♣ Q 10 7

**EAST**

♠ 9 7 4 2
♡ A K J 9 3 2
◊ 9 3
♣ J

### SOUTH

♠ A K Q J 10 6 3
♡ 8 5
◊ K
♣ A K 3

West gets off to an excellent defense based upon the few meager clues available. The heart ruff can never be prevented. He forces declarer to ruff the heart at Trick 2 and deprives him of an entry that could be used later. As it happens declarer has twelve tricks but cannot cash them.

Declarer removes East's four pieces of trump before playing the ♣ A K. When the club suit fails to divide evenly there is only one thin hope remaining; a squeeze.

**Condition B.** West is known to be Busy in clubs. If he also holds the ♦ Q J, or any combination of six or more diamonds, he can be Squeezed.

**Condition L.** Declarer has lost a spade trick. He has twelve winners, but the diamond suit is blocked leaving him with only eleven: seven spades, one diamond, two clubs, and the heart ruff.

**Condition U.** West must be our victim. North holds the Upper hand on West. Diamonds are the double threat. A club in either the North or the South hand will do nicely as the single threat. In this unusual case the hand can be played as the First Entry Form (Positional or Automatic).

**Condition E.** Entry to the North hand can be obtained only by overtaking the ♦ K.

NORTH

♠
♡
♦ A 10
♣ 9

WEST

♠
♡
♦ Q J
♣ Q

EAST

♠
♡ J
♦ 9 3
♣

SOUTH

♠ 3
♡
♦ K
♣ 3

South runs out his trump suit as the Count Down. Here we have the squeeze ending. As South plays the ♠ 3, West is squeezed. Declarer has been watching for only one card, not the ♣ Q, but the last club. It is unimportant to know the denomination of the card. It is important to know that there is only one club outstanding. If it does not appear the ♦ K is overtaken.

Keep in mind the fact that not every squeeze you try is going to be successful. The Bridge expert is continually running out squeeze positions that fail because Condition B never existed. He realizes, however, there is nothing to lose and, if the cards happen to be situated just right, as they are this time, there is quite a bit to be gained.

## The Auction:

| NORTH | SOUTH | WEST | NORTH | EAST |
|-------|-------|------|-------|------|
| ♠ 6532 | 1 ◊ | 1 ♠ | Pass | Pass |
| ♡ 863 | 1 N.T. | Pass | Pass | Pass |
| ◊ 103 | | | | |
| ♣ K862 | Opening Lead: ♠ K | | | |

SOUTH

♠ A94
♡ AJ
◊ KQJ4
♣ A954

Trick 1: ♠K–2–7–4
Trick 2: ♠Q–3–A East ♡2
Trick 3: ◊4–6–10–2
Trick 4: ◊3–5–K–A
Trick 5: ♣J–5–9 East ♡4
Trick 6: ♣10–6 East ♡7 South ♣4
Trick 7: ♠8 No ♡3 East ♣3 So ♣5
Trick 8: ♡10 ?

**Plan your play at match-point Duplicate.**

NORTH

♠ 6532
♡ 863
◊ 103
♣ K862

WEST

♠ KQJ108
♡ 1095
◊ A876
♣ Q

EAST

♠ 7
♡ KQ742
◊ 952
♣ J1073

SOUTH

♠ A94
♡ AJ
◊ KQJ4
♣ A954

South is assured of seven tricks and his contract as soon as he drives out the opponent's ♦ A, but in tournament play an overtrick is very important.

**Condition B.** If East started with the ♥ K Q plus three or more clubs, he will fall victim to the squeeze machine.

**Condition L.** The defense has won five tricks. Declarer has seven winners out of the remaining eight tricks: The ♠ A, the ♥ A, three diamonds, and two top clubs.

**Condition U.** East is the hand to be squeezed. South holds the Upper hand on East. The single threat of the ♥ J fulfills U against East.

**Condition E.** The ♣ K is our entry to the double threat in dummy. When the ♥ J is in the South hand with the squeeze card we have the first Entry Form (Automatic).

South plays his diamond winners for the Count Down. This is the end position before the last diamond is played.

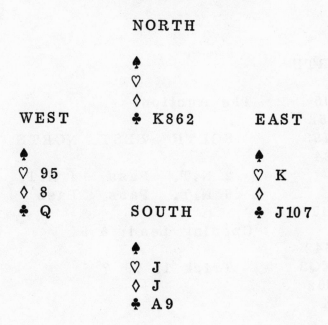

The play of the ♦ J squeezes East. Declarer watches for only one key card, the ♥ K. If it does not appear on or before the squeeze trick, the ♣ A K are played ending in dummy.

NORTH

♠ KJ5
♡ 1052
◊ QJ93
♣ Q84

SOUTH

♠ A542
♡ AKQ3
◊ K102
♣ AK

The Auction:

| SOUTH | WEST | NORTH | EAST |
|-------|------|-------|------|
| 2 N.T. | Pass | 4 N.T. | Pass |
| 6 N.T. | Pass | Pass | Pass |

Opening Lead: ♠ 9

Trick 1: ♠9 ?

Plan your play.

## NORTH

♠ KJ3
♡ 1052
◊ QJ93
♣ Q84

WEST

♠ 987
♡ 7
◊ 865
♣ J97632

EAST

♠ Q106
♡ J9864
◊ A74
♣ 105

## SOUTH

♠ A542
♡ AKQ3
◊ K102
♣ AK

The **S** 9 opening lead should be accepted as evidence that the ⊤ Q lies with RHO, and any attempt at a finesse is doomed to failure. This leaves declarer with four possible ways to bring home this contract: the hearts may divide evenly, the ♥ J may lie singleton or doubleton in a defender's hand, the opening lead may have been from ♠ 9 8 7 2 in which case East's ♠ Q 10 doubleton will fall under our ♠ A K, or East may hold the ♠ Q plus four or more hearts headed by the ♥ J and is subject to a squeeze. In playing this hand South must allow for each of these possibilities, but first let's examine the BLUE Law.

**Condition B.** We hope that East holds the ♠ Q and four or more hearts to the ♥ J.

**Condition L.** After the ♦ A is lost Declarer has two spades, three hearts, three diamonds, and three clubs. With one trick lost to the ♦ A, Condition L is in order.

**Condition U.** South has the Upper hand on East. The heart suit is a double threat in the Upper hand to satisfy U.

**Condition E.** This hand represents the First Entry Form (Automatic). However, it is the first hand you have seen with the squeeze card in dummy.

# THE SIMPLE SQUEEZE IN BRIDGE

Everything will seem to work upside-down.

To preserve every one of the four possibilities discussed previously, declarer must play each suit in its proper order. Trick 1 is taken in the closed hand with the ♠ A. Diamonds are played with East offering the best defense by holding off until the third round. The club or heart return is won by South. Two rounds of hearts are played looking for the ♥ J. When it fails to appear, South cashes the ♠ A K, leaving this ending.

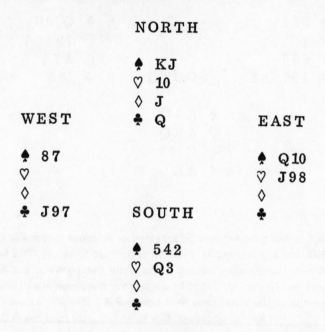

NORTH

♠ K J
♡ 10
◊ J
♣ Q

WEST

♠ 8 7
♡
◊
♣ J 9 7

EAST

♠ Q 10
♡ J 9 8
◊
♣

SOUTH

♠ 5 4 2
♡ Q 3
◊
♣

Declarer crosses to dummy's ♠ K. The ♦ J and the ♣ Q are played from the North hand in any order as the ♠ 5 4 serve as free discards from the closed hand. East has an extra heart which is an Idle card. It can be discarded to the first play from dummy, but the second trick executes the squeeze.

NORTH        The Auction:

♠ KQ63       SOUTH    WEST    NORTH    EAST
♡ A963
◊ J54        1 N.T.    Pass    2 ♣     Pass
♣ 82         2 ♡       Pass    4 ♡     Pass
             Pass      Pass


SOUTH        Opening Lead: ♡ 8

♠ A5         Trick 1: ♡8-3-K-2
♡ QJ102      Trick 2: ♣Q-K-A-2
◊ AK82       Trick 3: ♣9-8-5-4
♣ K64        Trick 4: ♡5 ?

Plan your play.

NORTH

♠ KQ63
♡ A963
◇ J54
♣ 82

WEST

♠ J984
♡ 85
◇ Q973
♣ A93

EAST

♠ 1072
♡ K74
◇ 106
♣ QJ1075

SOUTH

♠ A5
♡ QJ102
◇ AK82
♣ K64

Declarer has managed to lose the first three tricks on this deal by unlucky finesses in both trumps and clubs. There are two slim possibilities left to fulfill this contract. If the ◆ Q is either singleton or doubleton or if the ◆ Q and spade length are held by West, a squeeze can be developed.

**Condition B.** For our squeeze to work, we must assume the ◆ Q and four or more spades are held by West.

**Condition L.** We have lost the first three tricks. There are ten remaining. We have nine winners: three spades, three hearts, two diamonds, and a club ruff in dummy.

**Condition U.** The spades in dummy are a double threat. The ◆ J will be a single threat after the ◆ A K have been played. The ◆ 8 held by South can be used as a single menace against East, but only if he started with four or more, or if he holds specifically the ◆ Q 10 9.

**Condition E.** Spades supply the entry to the ◆ J if West is squeezed by the Third Entry Form (Positional). The ◆ 8 gives us a First Entry Form (Automatic) Squeeze against East, if he has the right diamond holding.

After winning West's lead at Trick 4, declarer plays the hand as follows while watching every diamond discard. A third round of hearts is won in the closed hand and the last club is trumped on the table. West has parted with a diamond on our third round of trump. The ♦ A K are next as both opponents follow suit. The ♦ Q is the only outstanding card in the suit as we reach this squeeze ending.

```
                    NORTH

                    ♠ KQ63
                    ♡
                    ◊ J
     WEST           ♣              EAST

  ♠ J984                         ♠ 1072
  ♡                              ♡
  ◊ Q                            ◊
  ♣               SOUTH          ♣ J10

                    ♠ A5
                    ♡ 10
                    ◊ 82
                    ♣
```

South plays his squeeze card, the ♥ 10. West is Squeezed Positionally since he must discard before the dummy. If east had started with four spades plus four diamonds, the squeeze would have been automatic with the ♦ 8 as the single menace. If East had specifically the ♦ Q 10 9 our squeeze would also have succeeded.

## Chapter III

# Developing The Conditions Of The BLUE Law

In the Examples and Problem Hands presented so far you have only to discover the four conditions of the BLUE Law and play the cards out in their proper order to be rewarded when the squeeze machine produced its one trick profit. Unfortunately, not every squeeze hand is dealt in perfect working order. Some adjusting or rearranging may be necessary before the squeeze will operate properly and provide the desired result.

Of the four conditions in the BLUE Law, B, L, and U are subject to being developed or improved upon by declarer, providing the proper raw materials are present with which to work. E is the only one that resists being changed, adjusted, transferred, or rearranged to better suit declarer's purpose. To describe condition E in the vernacular of Damon Runyon, "You either got it baby, or you ain't."

We will consider B, L, and U in the order of frequency normally encountered in play instead of their natural order.

# Developing Condition L

A beginning bridge player does everything he possibly can to keep from losing a single trick. We have all watched the tyro cash out every high card in his hand and then lead an unprotected king in hopes that the defender holding the Ace is either a benevolent soul or fast asleep.

As the novice gains experience he is not so quick to play off all of his winners but he still lacks the judgement needed to examine each hand and estimate its maximum potential. On the other hand, the expert is well aware of the trick taking limitations of every hand he holds. He also knows how his cards must be played in order to produce that extra trick out of what would seem to be thin air. His two favorite weapons are end plays. One is the Throw-in; the other is the Squeeze.

The throw-in works best when Declarer has winners for all but two of the remaining tricks. A defender is then given the lead with one of these two tricks. His forced return gives declarer either a free finesse or a sluff and ruff for a one trick profit.

A simple squeeze employs a slightly different technique. Declarer must be only one trick away from winning the balance of the tricks in hand. Pressure is then applied to a single defender causing him to make a forced discard, which provides Declarer with an extra trick.

If you intend employing a Throw-in ending, you had best reduce yourself to within two tricks of your remaining total number of winners. If you wish to develop a Squeeze, you must reduce your hand to an outstanding loser count of one.

### Rectifying the Count

A simple squeeze is a pressure play. It is designed to gain one trick in addition to the natural tricks you can take with your high card winners. For a squeeze to work, your opponent must be restricted in the number of Idle cards he holds in his hand. One Idle card held by your intended victim at the time you play your squeeze card destroys any chance of executing the squeeze.

With the exception of Illustration (F) and Example (9) in Chapter I, every Illustration, Example, and Problem Hand you have seen so far has been presented with Condition L in good working order. In actual play this is not usually the case.

As declarer, it is considered good general practice to reduce yourself to a throw-in or squeeze position early in the play of any hand, while you still are in control of all suits. This can be done by ducking the opening lead and a defender's subsequent continuations until the desired position is reached. Another method is to win a trick at the earliest opportunity, extract trump if need be, and then give up the prerequisite number of tricks until the desired end position is reached.

### NORTH

♠ Q6
♡ A94
◊ A832
♣ A852

| WEST | | EAST |
|---|---|---|
| ♠ K87532 | | ♠ A1094 |
| ♡ 8532 | | ♡ 7 |
| ◊ J7 | | ◊ 10954 |
| ♣ 3 | **SOUTH** | ♣ J1097 |

♠ J
♡ KQJ106
◊ KQ6
♣ KQ64

## The Auction:

| NORTH | EAST | SOUTH | WEST |
|---|---|---|---|
| 1 ◊ | Pass | 1 ♡ | Pass |
| 2 ♡ | Pass | 3 ♣ | Pass |
| 4 ♣ | Pass | 4 N.T. | Pass |
| 5 ♠ | Pass | 6 ♡ | Pass |
| Pass | Pass | | |

Opening Lead: ♣ 3

# THE SIMPLE SQUEEZE IN BRIDGE

West leads the ♣3 against a contract of 6 ♥. South wins the first trick in his hand with the ♣ K and draws the adverse trump in four rounds, pitching a spade from the North hand. East must find three discards. They should all be spades. It is at this point that many declarers go wrong. They immediately run the diamond suit, hoping that diamonds will provide a place to discard the ♠ J. Now the hand can no longer be made.

The proper line of play after eliminating the adverse trump is to lead the ♣ Q, not diamonds. If the outstanding clubs are divided three-two, South tries a spade-diamond squeeze by running all of his club and heart winners. If the ♠ A K plus four or more diamonds are in either opponent's hand, he will be Squeezed for the overtrick; if the diamonds divided three-three all the time, nothing has been lost.

As the cards lie, West fails to follow to the second trick in clubs. The success or failure of this hand would seem now to depend upon an even division of the diamond suit. There is, however, an additional possibility. East is known to have started with four clubs. If he also holds four or more diamonds, he can be squeezed. Here is our present position.

### NORTH

♠ Q  
♡  
◊ A 8 3 2  
♣ A 8

### WEST

♠ K 8 7 5 3  
♡  
◊ J 7  
♣

### EAST

♠ A  
♡  
◊ 10 9 5 4  
♣ J 10

### SOUTH

♠ J  
♡ 10  
◊ K Q 6  
♣ 6 4

South has five winners with seven tricks remaining. Condition L is not in order. If the squeeze card, the ♥ 10, is played now, East is forced to throw away his ♠ A in order to protect his minor suit holdings. By doing so he will eventually beat the contract. However, if, at this point, declarer rectifies the count by leading his ♠ J, the hand can be made by squeezing RHO.

East wins the ♠ A and returns a diamond. A club would be no better. The trick is won in the closed hand and the ♣ A is cleared. A diamond return to South brings about this end position.

```
                      NORTH
                        ♠
                        ♡
                        ◇ A 8
        WEST            ♣ 8            EAST
        ♠ K 8 7                        ♠
        ♡                              ♡
        ◇                              ◇ 10 9
        ♣            SOUTH             ♣ J
                        ♠
                        ♡ 10
                        ◇ 6
                        ♣ 6
```

Now that we have rectified the count, the ♥ 10 is led. Dummy sheds the ♣ 8. Without an Idle card to serve as a free discard East is squeezed between the ♣ 6 in the closed hand and the ♦ A 8 in dummy.

In Example (10) declarer could have rectified the count at Trick 2 by playing his singleton ♠ J. This is a risky procedure at a trump contract and in this case would have led to defeat. East wins his ♠ A and gives his partner a club ruff. Therefore, the earliest point in the hand at which a spade trick can be surrendered is after the outstanding trumps have been drawn. Depending on the existing circumstances, you must select just the right moment at which to bring yourself down to a one-more-loser situation.

## NORTH

♠ A J 10 8
♡ A K 4 2
◇ 9 4
♣ A K 6

## WEST

♠ 9 3
♡ J 8 7 3
◇ J 10 8
♣ J 9 7 4

## EAST

♠ 7 5 4 2
♡ 9 5
◇ K Q 7 3 2
♣ 5 2

## SOUTH

♠ K Q 6
♡ Q 10 6
◇ A 6 5
♣ Q 10 8 3

The Auction:

| NORTH | EAST | SOUTH | WEST |
|-------|------|-------|------|
| 1 ♣ | Pass | 2 N.T. | Pass |
| 4 N.T. | Pass | 5 N.T. | Pass |
| 6 N.T. | Pass | Pass | Pass |

Opening Lead: ◇ J

This is just the type of hand on which the bridge expert shines, and the beginner is made to look so bad. At first glance the hand looks deceptively easy. If either clubs or hearts divide three-three, or if the jack of either suit is singleton or doubleton in a defender's hand, twelve winners are easily available. Also, if each suit produces four tricks, an overtrick can be made. The greenhorn wins Trick 1 with the ♦ A and attacks each suit in turn. When nothing divides evenly and no Jacks fall singleton or doubleton, he sheepishly surrenders the last two tricks. Down one.

Mr. Bridge Expert employs a line of play not too difficult from the tyro but with one important exception. He is much more interested in making his contract than in the possible overtrick. Therefore, he concedes Trick 1 to his adversaries. This gives him an additional chance to land his slam if a squeeze should prove necessary. Notice the importance of losing this trick immediately. There is no way to win the first trick and then rectify the count at a later date.

Now let's consider the play. Trick 2 is taken with the ♦ A. The heart suit comes next, first the ♥ Q and then the ♥ A. When the ♥ J fails to appear, the ♥ K is tried looking for the three-three split. When this fails, our four spade winners are run. This is the end position as the last spade is played from dummy.

```
                    NORTH

                    ♠ J
                    ♡ 4
                    ◊
         WEST       ♣ AK6        EAST

         ♠                       ♠ 7
         ♡ J                     ♡
         ◊                       ◊ KQ
         ♣ J974     SOUTH        ♣ 52

                    ♠
                    ♡
                    ◊ 6
                    ♣ Q1083
```

The ♠ J is led and the ♦ 6 is played from the closed hand. West is squeezed. This squeeze will not operate if declarer wins the opening lead. West would be left with an Idle card to use as a discard when the squeeze card is played.

This becomes a more delicate problem in match-point play where there is a great premium on producing an overtrick. If both red suits behave, 13 tricks are there for the taking, and you will be rewarded with a be-low-average score for your fine technique.

## The Theory of Maximum Pressure

On any given deal of cards, squeeze hand or otherwise, pressure can only be brought to bear against your opponents after eliminating their Idle cards. As a matter of general principle, you should contrive to let the enemy win exactly the right number of tricks to suit your own purpose. By reducing your loser count to within one or two tricks of your winners, you not only cause squeeze and throw-in situations to exist, you create a climate in which your opponents stand the best chance of making a mistake. Notice the thrust and counterthrust on the next hand.

NORTH

♠ 965
♡ 1062
◊ AJ4
♣ AK82

WEST

♠ Q743
♡ KQJ9
◊ 76
♣ 1063

EAST

♠ J102
♡ 75
◊ Q1095
♣ J754

SOUTH

♠ AK8
♡ A843
◊ K832
♣ Q9

The Auction:

| SOUTH | WEST | NORTH | EAST |
|-------|------|--------|------|
| 1 N.T. | Pass | 3 N.T. | Pass |
| Pass | Pass | | |

Opening Lead: ♡ K

Declarer holds off on the ♥ A until the third round. Already, RHO is in difficulty. Keeping clubs is obvious, but the choice between spades and diamonds is not altogether clear. Let's presume he makes the correct decision and throws the ♠ 2. Our contract would seem to hinge on producing three tricks from the diamond suit. With this in mind, the finesse is taken to the ♦ which loses. East exits with the ♠ J. As South wins the ♠ A, the theory of maximum pressure comes to mind, and he decides to reduce is loser count to one by giving West his Heart winner arriving at the following position.

```
                    NORTH

                 ♠ 96
                 ♡
                 ◊ A4
    WEST         ♣ AK82         EAST

 ♠ Q74                       ♠ 10
 ♡ 9                         ♡
 ◊ 7                         ◊ 1095
 ♣ 1063          SOUTH       ♣ J754

                 ♠ K8
                 ♡ 8
                 ◊ K83
                 ♣ Q9
```

South plays the ♥ 8 and eliminates a small spade from dummy. East's hand continues to compress. He is forced to release his last Idle card, the ♠ 10. Maximum pressure has been brought to bear. With the ♠ 10 gone West cannot play the suit without presenting declarer with his ninth trick. And yet he cannot be sure that the play of either minor suit will not put his partner to a finesse. The play of a small club would put an end to all defensive chances. Assuming West makes the correct choice of either the ♦ 7 or the ♠ 10, the hand can still be brought to this conclusion.

NORTH

♠ 9
♡
◊
♣ AK8

WEST

♠ Q7
♡
◊
♣ 63

EAST

♠
♡
◊ 10
♣ J75

SOUTH

♠ K8
♡
◊ 8
♣ 9

Declarer leads the ♠ K and RHO is Squeezed. Allowing West to win his heart tricks rather than trying to prevent him from doing so not only gave the defense the greatest opportunity to make an error, but it also rectified the count for an eventual squeeze against East.

### NORTH

♠ 843
♡ K10 5 4
◊ A 10 9
♣ 942

### WEST

♠ A J 9 6 2
♡ J 8
◊ 8 7 4 2
♣ J 3

### EAST

♠ Q 7
♡ Q 9 7 6 2
◊ 6 5 3
♣ Q 10 7

### SOUTH

♠ K 10 5
♡ A 3
◊ K Q J
♣ A K 8 6 5

## The Auction:

| SOUTH | WEST | NORTH | EAST |
|-------|------|-------|------|
| 1 ♣ | Pass | 1 ♡ | Pass |
| 2 N.T. | Pass | 3 N.T. | Pass |
| Pass | Pass | | |

## Opening Lead: ♠ 6

South takes the ♠ K at Trick 1 and can count only eight winners. Assuming a normal distribution of the outstanding clubs, a long suit winner can be established by giving up a trick in the suit. However, spades represent a clear and present danger. West may have started with a five-card suit. In the process of establishing a ninth trick for ourselves we give up the lead to the enemy, and they promptly defeat our contract.

Applying the theory of maximum pressure, our proper play at Trick 2 is a spade. If LHO started with five, RHO had only two and we have succeeded is severing communication in the suit. West may cash his four winners, but now we have a chance for a club-heart squeeze against East. This is the situation after West has run his spade winners.

```
                    NORTH
                    ♠
                    ♡ K 10 5
                    ◇ A 10 9
          WEST      ♣ 94          EAST
          ♠                       ♠
          ♡ J 8                   ♡ Q 9 7
          ◇ 8 7 4 2               ◇ 6 5
          ♣ J 3     SOUTH         ♣ Q 10 7
                    ♠
                    ♡ A 3
                    ◇ K Q J
                    ♣ A K 8
```

West can return any suit. South wins and cashes out the ♥ A K stablishing the ♥ 10 as a single menace. Three rounds of diamonds squeezes East.

If West had only four spades to start with, or if he had five and refuses to cash the last one to keep his partner off the squeeze (nice defensive try), we have this situation.

NORTH

♠  
♡ K 10 5 4  
◊ A 10 9  
♣ 94  

WEST

♠ 2  
♡ J8  
◊ 8742  
♣ J3  

EAST

♠  
♡ Q976  
◊ 65  
♣ Q 10 7  

SOUTH

♠  
♡ A3  
◊ KQJ  
♣ AK86  

South wins any return, cashes the ♣ A K, and gives a club trick to East. West has the setting trick in spades but cannot gain the lead to cash it.

This process by which one defender runs a suit, thereby rectifying the count for an eventual squeeze against his own partner is sometimes referred to as a Suicide Squeeze. *

# Developing Condition B

Condition B may actually be caused to exist in a hand that does not contain the condition in its natural state. The two methods by which this can be accomplished are known as *Isolating the Menace* and *Transferring the Menace*. Isolating the menace is the much more common practice of the two. Hands on which you have an opportunity to transfer a menace are rare.

### Isolating the Menace

On occasion both opponents will hold length in the same suit. This prevents declarer from using a small card in the suit as a menace against either defender.

*This does not meet the specifications as outlined in the "Encyclopedia of Bridge" and is, therefore, a misnomer. See Chapter V for a true Suicide Squeeze.

                          NORTH

                          ♡ 63

        WEST                              EAST

        ♡ Q1082                           ♡ J74

                          SOUTH

                          ♡ AK95

As the cards lie in this illustration, both opponents can defend against the third round of hearts. A simple squeeze cannot be developed against either defender using this card combination as it now stands for a threat suit. Neither adversary fulfills the requirement for Condition B that, "One defender must have Busy cards in two suits while his partner is helpless."

In order for one defender to be naturally helpless in this suit he would have to hold less than three cards or be unable to best South's ♥ 9 with his highest card. When condition B fails to exist naturally, declarer may render one opponent helpless in the suit by removing his third round control. This leaves his partner to defend against the fourth card in the suit by himself.

With clubs as trump Declarer can lead out the ♥ A K and trump the third round. At No Trump, the menace may be isolated by leading a small card in the suit out from under the ♥ A K. Either play would leave West in sole control of the fourth heart. We now have a menace card. Remember, if one defender is not helpless in a suit, a threat cannot exist against the other.

NORTH

♠ 8 3
♡ 6 3
◊ K Q 5 3
♣ A K 10 4 3

WEST

♠ K Q
♡ Q 10 8 2
◊ J 9 7 4 2
♣ 9 2

EAST

♠ A J 10 7 6 2
♡ J 7 4
◊ 10
♣ 8 7 5

SOUTH

♠ 9 5 4
♡ A K 9 5
◊ A 8 6
♣ Q J 6

## The Auction:

| SOUTH | WEST | NORTH | EAST |
|-------|------|-------|------|
| 1 ♣ | Pass | 3 ♣ | Pass |
| 3 ♡ | Pass | 4 ♣ | Pass |
| 5 ♣ | Pass | Pass | Pass |

## Opening Lead: ♠ K

LHO holds Trick 1 with the ♠ K and continues with the ♠ Q. His partner overtakes to play back the singleton ♦ 10.

Declarer can count ten winners. He has a choice of two lines of play to produce an eleventh trick. For the first line of play two rounds of trump are pulled leaving a trump outstanding. Diamonds are now run. If the suit divides evenly or if four or more diamonds are located in the same hand with the remaining trump, a ruff in the closed hand will produce the game-going trick.

The second line of play involves a squeeze. Declarer removes all of the opposing trump before cashing the ♥ A K and ruffing a heart in dummy. Regardless of how the suit was divided to begin with only one defender now can protect against the remaining heart length card. If that same opponent holds four or more diamonds, he can be squeezed. This is our end position.

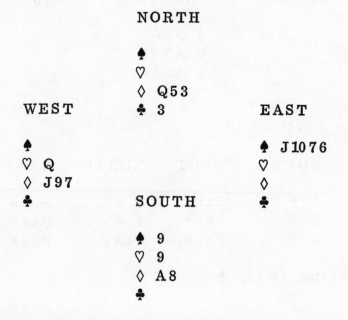

```
                     NORTH
                      ♠
                      ♡
                      ◊  Q 5 3
                      ♣  3
       WEST                           EAST
        ♠                              ♠  J 10 7 6
        ♡  Q                           ♡
        ◊  J 9 7                       ◊
        ♣               SOUTH          ♣
                         ♠  9
                         ♡  9
                         ◊  A 8
                         ♣
```

As North leads the ♣ 3, the ♠ 9 is discarded from the closed hand. West is squeezed by the Second Entry Form. It is important to note that had a heart not been ruffed in dummy, the ♥ J would still be in the East hand. Our squeeze would fail for lack of B.

NORTH

♠ 6432
♡ A2
◊ 984
♣ AQ62

WEST

♠ QJ1097
♡ 6
◊ AKQ6
♣ K87

EAST

♠ K85
♡ 8743
◊ 732
♣ 1093

SOUTH

♠ A
♡ KQJ10 95
◊ J105
♣ J54

The Auction:

| WEST | NORTH | EAST | SOUTH |
|------|-------|------|-------|
| 1 ♠ | Pass | Pass | 2 ♡ |
| Dbl. | Redbl. | 2 ♠ | 3 ♡ |
| 3 ♠ | 4 ♡ | Pass | Pass |
| Pass | | | |

Opening Lead: ◊ K

# THE SIMPLE SQUEEZE IN BRIDGE

An unfortunate duplication of distribution in diamonds allows LHO to win the first three tricks for the defense. At Trick 4 he shifts to the ♠ Q. This play would seem to indicate the ♠ K lies to the right. If this is so the ♣ K must be to our left. Surely, if both black Kings were in the East hand he would not have passed his partner's opening bid. With the club finesse a virtual certainty we can count one spade, six hearts, and two clubs for a total of nine winners. If the ♣ K is singleton or doubleton with West, there is no problem to the hand. But what if it isn't?

After we take the club finesse, we are left with the split threat position of ♣ A 6 opposite ♣ J 5. If a second menace can be developed in Dummy, West can be squeezed using the Third Entry Form. The only threat prospect in dummy is Spades, but East is sure to hold at least one and probably two cards higher than the lowly spot cards on board.

If LHO holds five spades and East only three, the size of North's spades will become immaterial. Spades can be ruffed twice after the ♠ A is gone and East becomes defenseless in the suit. Here is one successful line of play. I am sure you can find workable alternatives.

South wins Trick 4 with the ♠ A and enters dummy with the ♥ A. A spade is ruffed and the open hand is re-entered by finessing the ♣ Q. A second spade is trumped in the closed hand and trumps are played down to the last card to arrive at our squeeze ending.

NORTH

    ♠ 6
    ♡
    ◊
    ♣ A 6

WEST               EAST

♠ J                  ♠
♡                   ♡ 8
◊                   ◊
♣ K 8     SOUTH     ♣ 10 9

    ♠
    ♡ J
    ◊
    ♣ J 5

# THE SIMPLE SQUEEZE IN BRIDGE

South led his last heart. In addition to being a squeeze card against West, it also extracts the last outstanding trump from East. Trumping out two spades to create a single menace of dummy's remaining spot-card is not as exotic as it may seem. Disclosures made during the auction and the early play of this hand made the result an almost sure thing. Without the spade ruffs, East would be able to control the Spade suit and our squeeze would fail for lack of B.

<pre>
                        NORTH

                     ♠ A 9
                     ♡ 10 8 6 5
                     ◇ K 9 5 2
          WEST       ♣ A Q 4          EAST

      ♠ 10 5 2                     ♠ Q J 8 7
      ♡ 7 3 2                      ♡ K Q J 9
      ◇ 8 7 3                      ◇ J 4
      ♣ 8 6 5 3        SOUTH       ♣ K J 7

                     ♠ K 6 4 3
                     ♡ A 4
                     ◇ A Q 10 6
                     ♣ 10 9 2
</pre>

## The Auction:

| SOUTH | WEST | NORTH | EAST |
|-------|------|-------|------|
| 1 ◇ | Pass | 1 ♡ | Dbl. |
| 1 N.T. | Pass | 3 N.T. | Dbl. |
| Pass | Pass | Pass | |

## Opening Lead: ♡ 2

East's first double was for take-out, but the second one was business and requested his partner to lead the first bid suit by dummy, hearts.

East is allowed to hold the first heart trick. South wins the ♥ A when the suit is continued. At Trick 3, declarer makes the key play of a Spade to the ♠ 9 on the board. West can no longer control the third round of the suit. Spades have just become a defensive problem belonging exclusively to East. RHO completes the defensive book by cashing two good hearts before exiting with a small spade to dummy's ♠ A.

The Squeeze is not set. East is marked with four Spades and the ♣ K for his Take-Out Double. Declarer returns to his hand with the ♦ A and plays the ♠ K. This leaves the fourth spade as a single menace. The ♦ K is next leaving this four-card ending.

<pre>
                    NORTH
                    ♠
                    ♡
                    ◊ 9 5
      WEST          ♣ A Q          EAST
      ♠                            ♠ Q
      ♡                            ♡
      ◊ 8                          ◊
      ♣ 8 6 5       SOUTH          ♣ K J 7
                    ♠ 6
                    ♡
                    ◊ Q 10
                    ♣ 10
</pre>

We are one trick away from our squeeze. East has an idle card, the ♣ 7 to play on the ♦ Q, but the ♦ 10 completes the squeeze. East must either bare his ♣ K or throw the ♠ Q, establishing declarers small spade. Notice that if declarer had not surrendered an early spade trick, West would still have a spade guard and East could discard his ♠ Q as an Idle card. By surrendering an early spade, declarer Isolated the Menace.

This hand will come up for further analysis in Chapter VI.

### Transferring the Menace

Condition B may be manipulated in yet another manner. If the opposing cards are properly placed, the location of the Busy cards in a suit may be transferred from one opponent to the other. This is done so that one threat will reside in the same hand with another for a squeeze.

NORTH

♣ Q8

WEST      EAST

♣ J76532    ♣ K94

SOUTH

♣ A10

With clubs distributed in this manner declarer is in possession of a split threat. It can be used for a third entry form squeeze against East, or, if the ♣ A is played, the ♣ Q will serve as a single menace against either defender. This is all well and good if the ♣ K is in the same hand with the second menace. But what if it isn't? Let us suppose for the moment that West is suspected of holding one threat, but the ♣ K is known to be with East. No squeeze can exist. In this case, however, RHO can be relieved of his control of clubs by the simple expedient of playing the ♣ Q from dummy. East must cover with the ♣ K or lose the trick here and now. South takes the ♣ A and the ♣ 10 becomes a single menace against West's ♣ J. The menace has effectively been transferred from East to West.

### NORTH

♠ KQ83
♡ 982
◇ A643
♣ Q8

### WEST

♠
♡ 74
◇ J8752
♣ J76532

### EAST

♠ J974
♡ AKQ103
◇ 9
♣ K94

### SOUTH

♠ A10652
♡ J65
◇ KQ10
♣ A10

## The Auction:

| EAST | SOUTH | WEST | NORTH |
|------|-------|------|-------|
| 1 ♡ | 1 ♠ | Pass | 4 ♠ |
| Dbl. | Pass | Pass | Pass |

Opening Lead: ♡ 7

# THE SIMPLE SQUEEZE IN BRIDGE

It would seem that an unsound penalty double by East is about to pay off in a very small profit. Declarer's chances of bringing this contract home are not good. East wins the first three hearts and shifts to the ♦ 9. South must be careful not to try to finesse for the ♦ J. This would drive the ♦ A out of dummy and destroy condition E of our possible squeeze.

Declarer wins the ♦ K and plays a small spade to the North hand only to find the four missing trump are all to his right. This places four minor suit cards with RHO, three of which are unknown. LHO has eleven cards in the minors. This makes it impossible for the diamond suit to split three-three and provide a place to discard the ♣ 10.

West could be squeezed if he holds the ♣ K plus four or more diamonds, but this cannot be. East must have the ♣ K for his opening bid and subsequent penalty double. Condition B is not properly fulfilled.

There is a chance of making this hand, however, if East holds the ♣ K, and West holds the ♣ J. The club menace can be transferred from right to left by playing the ♣ Q. Here is the proper line of play from the point where declarer wins Trick 5 with the ♠ K. The finesse is taken against East's ♠ J and the remaining trump are extracted ending up in dummy. The ♣ Q is next. East must cover with the ♣ K and South wins the ♣ A. The ♣ 10 in the closed hand is now established as a single menace against West. This is the squeeze ending.

```
                    NORTH
                      ♠
                      ♡
                      ◊  A 6 4
     WEST             ♣  8          EAST
      ♠                              ♠
      ♡                              ♡  10 3
      ◊  J 8 7                       ◊
      ♣  J           SOUTH           ♣  9 4
                      ♠  6
                      ♡
                      ◊  Q 10
                      ♣  10
```

Declarer's last spade puts the squeeze to West.

## Using Trump to Transfer the Menace

It is possible to transfer a menace using trump as a base against which to operate. For example:

### NORTH

KJx

### SOUTH

Void

East is suspected of holding the ♥ A. Declarer plays the ♥ K forcing RHO to cover. The trick is ruffed and the ♥ J becomes a threat against the ♥ Q, which we hope is located to our left. Here are three other card combinations that lend themselves to being used in menace transfer situations involving the use of trump.


A Q 10           A K J 9           K Q 10

# THE SIMPLE SQUEEZE IN BRIDGE

It is rare, but not impossible, to find two honor cards fortunately placed for a trump menace transfer play. For example:

NORTH

Void

SOUTH

QJ9

Because of the auction, we have reason to suspect both the ♦ A and ♦ K are to our left, but the hand to be squeezed is to our right. First, the ♦ Q and then the ♦ J are played forcing West to cover each time. It is hoped that the ♦ 9 is now established as a single threat against East's ♦ 10. Here are other card combinations that lend themselves to this double transfer play.

A J 10 8          K J 9          K Q 10 8

You will find that additional one and two card transfer combinations become available once the suit has been played by an opponent.

NORTH

♠ A52
♡ K109
◊ QJ4
♣ AK65

WEST

♠ KQ
♡ J642
◊ AK8
♣ J1073

EAST

♠ J7
♡ AQ8753
◊ 9765
♣ 9

SOUTH

♠ 1098643
♡
◊ 1032
♣ Q842

The Auction:

| EAST | SOUTH | WEST | NORTH |
|------|-------|------|-------|
| 2 ♡* | Pass | 4 ♡ | Dbl. |
| Pass | 4 ♠ | Dbl. | Pass |
| Pass | Pass | | |

\* Weak 2 Bid.

Opening Lead: ◊ K

West wins his two top diamonds. When his partner fails to high-low and indicate an ability to ruff he shifts to the ♥ 2. This is a fatal mistake, for without that play the hand cannot be made.

Declarer calls for the ♥ 9 from dummy and ruffs away RHO's **W**. The ♠ A and then another trump puts West back on lead. He gets out with his last diamond. Declarer would like to take out insurance against a possible bad break in clubs by developing a potential squeeze, but the menace situation is all wrong. East is sure to hold the ♥ A, but if the club length is anywhere it is to the left. East's play of the ♥ Q suggests that West holds the ♥ J. If that's the case, the proper play at this point is the ♥ K. RHO must cover, and the ♥ 10 becomes a single menace against LHO's ♥ J. The count down of the spade suit brings about this five-card ending.

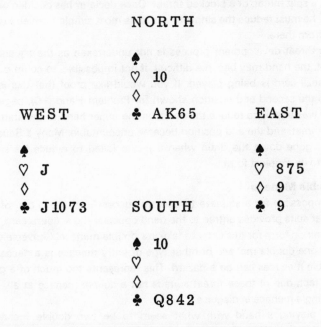

```
                        NORTH

                        ♠
                        ♡ 10
                        ◊
       WEST             ♣ AK65          EAST

       ♠                                ♠
       ♡ J                              ♡ 875
       ◊                                ◊ 9
       ♣ J1073          SOUTH           ♣ 9

                        ♠ 10
                        ♡
                        ◊
                        ♣ Q842
```

Declarer leads his last trump and discards Dummy's ♣ 5.
West is squeezed.

# Developing Condition U

To develop Condition U one has only to study the threat positions with relation to the opponent to be squeezed. After having rectified the count, a squeeze-oriented declarer goes about the business of isolating a menace if both defenders can protect the same suit, transferring a menace if one needs to be transferred, and reducing his menace positions to their most simple form. This may require that a more complex threat position be reduced to a more recognizable and easily handled form.

## The Single Menace

The single menace is the most important component in any squeeze hand. The single menace suit is the one declarer must count. It can be very elusive and camouflaged in a variety of ways, thereby becoming difficult to locate and recognize. Usually it stands disguised as some other form of menace. Declarer must analyze the hand, locate the fugitive single menace, and expose it for what it really is by cashing the other winners in the same suit. A single threat may lie under cover as a double menace, a compound menace, a split threat, or a blocked threat. Once declarer has decided on his squeeze, he must reduce the single threat to its most simple form and count the suit from there.

If this threat development process is not undertaken as the squeeze is being set, the hand may become difficult, if not impossible, to count out as the squeeze card is being played. If you would like proof that this is so, return to the second end position shown for Problem Hand (10), page Declarer was unable to reduce the hearts in the upper hand to the status of a single threat, and the end position became uncountable. Many a Squeeze hand has gone down the drain when a player failed to reduce his single menace to its simplest form.

## The Double Menace

It is impossible for a squeeze to operate successfully unless one of the two threat suits provides entree to the hand opposite the squeeze card. The most common form for this entry to take is a double menace. Conversely, as much as one double menace or other type of entry menace is a necessity, two double menaces can be a hazard. This represents too much of a good thing. In fact, one of these threat suits is not a double menace at all. It is really a single menace in disguise.

When playing a hand with what seem to be two double menaces, examine them carefully. If you were to cash the winning entry card or cards in either suit, where would the remaining single menace be? If it resides in the same hand with the squeeze card, that is the one to cash and reduce to a single threat. If both double menaces lie in the hand opposite the squeeze card, it is most important that one suit be reduced to the status of a single threat in the upper hand when looking for a First Entry Form (Positional) squeeze against the hand to the left of the squeeze card. Counting problems will arise if you don't make this a part of setting your squeeze and before beginning your count down. If both double threats lie in the same hand with the squeeze card, you cannot have a squeeze. *

## The Compound Menace

What looks like a compound threat often turns out not to be one at all. In Example (1 8), page    , the club suit is a true compound threat. It supplies entree to Dummy and the single menace plus a return entry to the closed hand. On the other hand the diamond suit in Example (1 7), page    , is not a compound menace. True, it supplies entries to both hands, but if the ♦ K Q were played, we would be left with a standard double menace. The true test of a compound threat is the location of the length threat.

It must be in the same hand with the squeeze card.

## The Split Threat

A split threat often resembles a tenace position. It is a difficult combination of cards to work with when setting up a squeeze for the simple reason that it can only be used for a Third Entry Form (Positional) squeeze against the hand to the left of the squeeze card, or in the Fourth Entry Form by reducing the holding to that of a blocked threat. This you will see later in Chapter V. Whenever possible, it is best to cash the high card winner in a split threat suit and use the remaining single threat plus a second menace for your squeeze. This is of particular importance for the Vienna Coup, which we will take up shortly.

## The Blocked Threat

A blocked menace is even more difficult to work with, than a split threat. It is usable in its natural state for only one type of Squeeze, and that is the Criss-Cross Squeeze or Fourth Entry Form. When at all possible, it is best to cash out the blocking winner and use the remaining threat in the opposite hand as a single menace.

To sum it up, you must be thoroughly familiar with the four conditions of the BLUE Law and the four Entry Forms before you will be able to recognize your menace positions and how to use them to your best advantage in developing a squeeze. Decide which threats to use, who to use them against, and then reduce them to their simplest form before beginning the count down.

*See Rule 1, Chapter I.

### NORTH

♠ J52
♡ K86
◇ A862
♣ Q82

WEST                          EAST

♠ 8764                        ♠ KQ10
♡ A7                          ♡ 10942
◇ Q9743                       ◇ J10
♣ 107        SOUTH           ♣ J963

♠ A93
♡ QJ53
◇ K5
♣ AK54

## The Auction:

| SOUTH | WEST | NORTH | EAST |
|-------|------|-------|------|
| 1 N.T. | Pass | 3 N.T. | Pass |
| Pass | Pass | | |

## Opening Lead: ♠ 8

# THE SIMPLE SQUEEZE IN BRIDGE

   Declarer arrives at a routine contract of 3 NT. West elects to employ a passive defense by leading the ♠ 8. South holds off until the third round not knowing that he could block the suit by winning the first or second trick. After taking the ♠ A, South establishes his heart winners by playing small to the ♥ K in dummy and back again to his ♥ J. West takes his ♥ A and the thirteenth spade which gives the defense four tricks. Everyone at the table discards a diamond on West's spade. This diamond discard from the South hand is very important. It allows declarer to maintain length threats in both clubs and hearts. West leads the ♦ 4, (a club would be no better), which is won in the closed hand by the ♦ K. A club to Dummy leaves the following 5 card ending.

NORTH

♠
♡ 8
♦ A 8
♣ 8 2

WEST

♠
♡
♦ Q 9 7 3
♣ 10

EAST

♠
♡ 10 9
♦
♣ J 9 6

SOUTH

♠
♡ Q 5
♦
♣ A K 5

   Here we have a perfect example of how not to operate a squeeze. The ♦ A is played and East releases a small club. Without a single threat to count there is no way of telling which suit is now established. RHO is known to have started with a total of eight cards between the club and heart suits. Were they originally four-four, and East has been squeezed; or did the hand to your right start with five clubs and three hearts in which case the heart suit was divided three-three all the time? The way this hand was played there is no way of telling. South has put himself to a guess.

# THE SIMPLE SQUEEZE IN BRIDGE

This situation should never have come to pass. Declarer could have set up his squeeze so there would have been absolutely no guesswork. Ironically, he had a choice of two lines of play.

After winning the ♦ K, he could try the ♥ Q to see if the suit splits three-three. When this fails, dummy is entered with the ♣ Q leaving this squeeze position.

### NORTH

♠  
♡  
♦ A 8  
♣ 8 2

WEST                                        EAST

♠                                           ♠  
♡                                           ♡ 10  
♦ Q 9 7                                     ♦  
♣ 10            SOUTH                        ♣ J 9 6

♠  
♡ 5  
♦  
♣ A K 5

East is known to hold an outstanding heart. If he fails to part with it as the ♦ A is played, the ♥ 5 is released from the closed hand and the ♣ A K 5 are all winners.

After winning the ♦ K, declarer has a second line of play. He can test the club suit by playing three winning rounds ending up with the ♣ Q on the board, which brings about this situation.

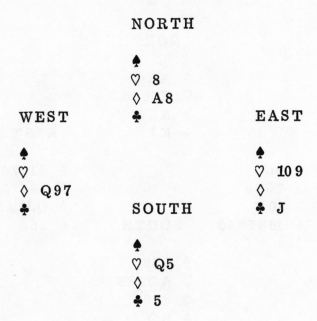

NORTH

♠
♡ 8
◇ A 8
♣

WEST                                          EAST

♠                                             ♠
♡                                             ♡ 10 9
◇ Q 9 7                                       ◇
♣                SOUTH                        ♣ J

♠
♡ Q 5
◇
♣ 5

This time RHO is known to hold the only remaining guard card in clubs. If he does not discard the ♣ J as the ♦ A is played, South gets rid of the ♣ 5. In each of these last two endings East's complete hand is known to declarer, thanks to his foresight in creating a single menace to count in the Upper hand.

### The Vienna Coup

One of the most exotic phrases in all of bridge, a term that finds its way into the vocabulary of all beginning bridge players long before they understand its meaning, is the Vienna Coup. From the time a novice first takes up the game, he looks forward to the day when he will learn to master this advanced playing technique. And now, after the aura of greatness, what a disappointment it is to find that a Vienna Coup is actually nothing more than an unblocking play for a simple squeeze. An important unblocking play to be sure, for without it the squeeze will not work. The Vienna Coup is a method for the development of Condition U.

### NORTH

♠ AKQ8
♡ K1096
♢ AK5
♣ KJ

### WEST

♠ 96
♡ 7543
♢ 10
♣ 1087642

### EAST

♠ J1074
♡
♢ QJ7432
♣ 953

### SOUTH

♠ 532
♡ AQJ82
♢ 986
♣ AQ

## The Auction:

| NORTH | EAST | SOUTH | WEST |
|-------|------|-------|------|
| 2 N.T. | Pass | 3 ♡ | Pass |
| 3 ♠* | Pass | 4 N.T. | Pass |
| 5 ♡ | Pass | 5 N.T. | Pass |
| 6 ♣ | Pass | 7 ♡ | Pass |
| Pass | Pass | | |

\* A Cue-Bid denoting the ♠ A, a
Heart fit, and slam interest.

Opening Lead: ♡ 3

# THE SIMPLE SQUEEZE IN BRIDGE

South bids a Grand Slam hoping to find at least three clubs in dummy. Thirteen tricks would then be easy. As it is, the hand seems to depend upon a three-three division of the spade suit. When declaring a hand like this, it should become second nature for you to look for an additional chance to make your contract. Examine the cards for any possible squeeze.

Three top spades could be cashed after trump has been drawn. This gives a Positional Squeeze against LHO, if he holds the fourth spade plus either the ♦ Q J 10 or any five or more diamonds. This squeeze will not work against East. Dummy would be forced to discard before a Busy RHO.

East can be squeezed if he is Busy in diamonds and spades only by using the Vienna Coup. Trumps are drawn in four rounds, and the ♦ A K are cleared from dummy. This unblocking play establishes the ♦ 9 as a single menace against RHO. Two rounds of clubs are then cashed ending in the closed hand to arrive at our squeeze position.

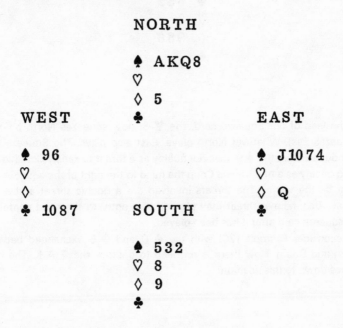

NORTH

♠ AKQ8
♡
♦ 5
♣

WEST

♠ 96
♡
♦
♣ 1087

EAST

♠ J1074
♡
♦ Q
♣

SOUTH

♠ 532
♡ 8
♦ 9
♣

South leads the ♥ 8 and eliminates the ♦ 5 from North. East is Squeezed. If the ♦ A K had not been unblocked in the early play of the hand, our ending would look like this.

NORTH

♠ AKQ8
♡
◊ AK5
♣

WEST                             EAST

♠ 96                            ♠ J 10 7 4
♡                              ♡
◊ 10                          ◊ QJ7
♣ 10 8 7 6      SOUTH         ♣

♠ 5 3 2
♡ 8
◊ 9 8 6
♣

The lead of our Squeeze card, the ♥ 8, now squeezes North before it Squeezes East. Whatever North plays, East also plays. The Squeeze fails. Without an entry the ♦ 9 does not qualify as a threat to satisfy Condition U.

To qualify as a true Vienna Coup the hand to the right of the squeeze card must be the victim. The threats involved are a double threat and a split threat. Also, neither threat may provide a re-entry to the hand containing the squeeze card after it has been played.

Reconsider Example (20) with the ♠ Q and ♠ 5 exchanged between North and South. Now there is no need to unblock the ♦ A K. The hand comes down to this position.

```
                   NORTH

                   ♠ AK85
                   ♡
                   ◊ AK5
   WEST            ♣             EAST

   ♠ 96                          ♠ J1074
   ♡                             ♡
   ◊ 10                          ◊ QJ7
   ♣ 10876       SOUTH           ♣

                   ♠ Q32
                   ♡ 8
                   ◊ 986
                   ♣
```

As the ♥8 is played the ♠5 is thrown from dummy irrespective of East's discard. If East elects to discard a diamond, the ♦A K are played and the ♠ Q will still provide an entry to the closed hand to cash the ♦9. The success or failure of the hand does not depend upon clearing the ♦A K early in the play. Therefore, the ending does not qualify as a Vienna Coup.

### NORTH

♠ Q83
♡ AK32
◊ K9
♣ 8643

WEST

♠ J965
♡ Q1076
◊ 8742
♣ 9

EAST

♠ K74
♡ J98
◊
♣ AKQJ1072

### SOUTH

♠ A102
♡ 54
◊ AQJ10653
♣ 5

## The Auction:

| EAST | SOUTH | WEST | NORTH |
|------|-------|------|-------|
| 3 N.T.* | 4 ◊ | Pass | 5 ◊ |
| Pass | Pass | Pass | |

\* Gambling 3 N.T. - Running minor
suit plus 1st or 2nd round control
of one side suit.

Opening Lead: ♣ 9

Some squeeze hands require that declarer develop only one condition of BLUE, while other involve two. This hand comes from a Swiss Team-of-Four match and involves three separate and distinct processes: Rectifying the Count, Isolating the Menace, and Transferring the Menace.

By definition East must hold a solid club suit plus the ♠ K for his bid. This does not make him a likely candidate for a squeeze. If a squeeze is to be developed, it must be perpetrated against West. Declarer ruffs the second round of clubs with the ♦ J in an effort to give East the impression that his partner holds the **D 10** and that repeated club plays might produce a trump trick for the defense.

Declarer passes a heart to East and holds his breath. A heart return removes Condition E and destroys any possible squeeze. Ducking the heart trick is a must. It rectifies the count and also isolates the heart menace against West. RHO goes for the bait and continues clubs. South ruffs with the ♦ 10 and cashes the ♦ K 9 in dummy. Next comes the ♠ Q. East must cover and the ♠ A is taken in the closed hand bringing about this position.

NORTH

♠ 8 3
♡ A K 3
◇
♣ 8

WEST

♠ J
♡ Q 10 7
◇ 8 7
♣

EAST

♠ 7 4
♡ J 9
◇
♣ A K

SOUTH

♠ 10 2
♡ 5
◇ A Q 6
♣

The diamond suit is run as three black cards are jetisoned from the open hand. West follows to the first two diamond plays with his remaining small trump, but on the third one he is squeezed. Shortly after the hand was completed, a Kibitzer was heard to say, "Wouldn't it have been easier to run all the Diamonds, cash the ♥ A K, and throw East in with a club? He would be end-played and forced to return a Spade." The Kibitzer was correct.

This deal is offered only as an example of what can be accomplished through the techniques of developing B, L, and U.

## SUMMARY, CHAPTER III

This completes our discourse on the development of conditions B, L, and U. You should now be able to take any hand and, providing the raw materials are there to work with, generate a squeeze ending.

There is a considerable amount of material in this chapter. Such subjects as the Theory of Maximum Pressure and how to recognize and develop your threats are fundamental to understanding the entire subject of squeeze plays.

If you are in doubt about any area covered thus far, return to that subject and review the material before continuing.

## Chapter IV

# Intermediate Problem Hands

Until now every problem hand you have seen was dealt with a squeeze all ready to go. Once you located your threats, all that had to be done was play out your winners in the proper order to reach the desired squeeze position. Unfortunately, all squeeze plays are not that easy.

With the knowledge you have gained in the previous chapter, you should now be able to develop conditions B, L, and U in hands that are not dealt all set to go so as to arrive at the proper squeeze ending.

Study each set of North-South hands and the information given. Decide for yourself what must be done with each hand to bring BLUE into line. You now have the knowledge. Let's put it to work.

NORTH    The Auction:

♠ Q84      SOUTH   WEST   NORTH   EAST
♡ 852
◊ A954     2 N.T.   Pass    6 N.T.   Pass
♣ AQ8      Pass    Pass

         Opening Lead: ♡ Q.

SOUTH
         Trick 1: ♡Q-2-4-A
♠ AK        Trick 2: ◊K-8-4-3
♡ AK6       Trick 3: ◊Q-5-7 West ♠2
◊ KQ62     Trick 4: ?
♣ K654

Plan your play.

### NORTH

♠ Q 8 4
♡ 8 5 2
◇ A 9 5 4
♣ A Q 8

WEST                                              EAST

♠ 9 7 6 5 3 2                  ♠ J 10
♡ Q J 10 3                       ♡ 9 7 4
◇ 8                                   ◇ J 10 7 3
♣ J 7                                ♣ 10 9 3 2

### SOUTH

♠ A K
♡ A K 6
◇ K Q 6 2
♣ K 6 5 4

At first glance there seems to be no problem on this deal. If both minor suits behave nicely, thirteen tricks are there for the taking. Declarer runs into difficulty at Trick 3. As he plays the ◇ K Q, West discards a spade on the second round.

The bad diamond split places the whole hand in jeopardy. If the clubs divide three-three, the hand can still be made. But what if they do not? Declarer should look for a possible squeeze position to serve as an additional safeguard, but who should be squeezed? If West holds five or more hearts plus four or more clubs, he will be Busy in two suits and can be squeezed. East may also be a candidate if he has four or more clubs to go with the four diamonds he is known to hold. Upon what do we base our decision?

If we play the ♠ A K the suit will still be under control with the ♠ Q in dummy. The opponents' discards may give us a clue. East plays the ♠ J 10 on these two tricks. Unless he is an extremely astute defender and has made a brilliant double false-card, his play indicates a shortness in spades. We should, therefore, select East to be our squeeze victim in the minor suits.

South can count only eleven winning tricks: three spades, two hearts, three diamonds, and three clubs. This is one loser away from our contract, but it is two losers away from the total number of tricks outstanding. A trick must be intentionally lost to bring condition L into line. Where can this best be done? In hearts and only in hearts. No other suit will do. A small heart should be given up now before losing control of any suit. Regardless of who wins the heart trick and which suit they return, this hand can be reduced to the following end position.

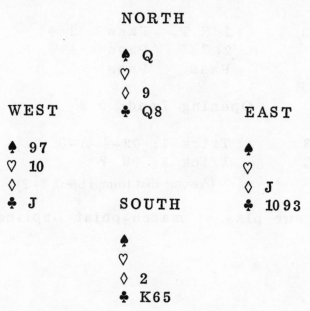

```
                    NORTH

                 ♠  Q
                 ♡
                 ◇  9
   WEST          ♣  Q8          EAST

 ♠  97                        ♠
 ♡  10                        ♡
 ◇                            ◇  J
 ♣  J           SOUTH         ♣  10 9 3

                 ♠
                 ♡
                 ◇  2
                 ♣  K 6 5
```

The lead can be in either hand. Declarer enters North with the ♣ Q and plays the ♠ Q.

East is squeezed.

The play of the small heart out from under the ♥ K has earned this type of hand a colorful name. It is known as a Submarine Squeeze.

## NORTH

♠ 864
♡ KQ64
◊ J4
♣ KQ63

### The Auction:

| SOUTH | WEST | NORTH | EAST |
|-------|------|-------|------|
| 1 N.T. | Pass | 2 ♣ | Pass |
| 2 ♡ | Pass | 4 ♡ | Pass |
| Pass | Pass | | |

## SOUTH

♠ KQ
♡ A953
◊ K653
♣ A52

### Opening Lead: ◊ 2

Trick 1: ◊2-4-A-3

Trick 2: ◊9 ?

(Assume that trumps break 3–2)

**Plan your play at match-point Duplicate.**

NORTH

♠ 8 6 4
♡ K Q 6 4
♢ J 4
♣ K Q 6 3

WEST

♠ A J 10
♡ 10 7
♢ Q 10 7 2
♣ 10 8 7 4

EAST

♠ 9 7 5 3 2
♡ J 8 2
♢ A 9 8
♣ J 9

SOUTH

♠ K Q
♡ A 9 5 3
♢ K 6 5 3
♣ A 5 2

North-South make use of the Stayman convention to reach a final contract of 4 ♥. At match-point duplicate it is important that they make as many overtricks as possible, but watch out, this deal is deceiving. It would appear there are only two losers on this hand, the ♦ A and the ♠ A. But, unless Declarer is an accomplished squeeze technician and plays his cards in their proper order, he is going to take only ten tricks with this hand and not eleven.

There are three separate and distinct tasks that South must attend to as he plays out his cards. He must draw trumps, force the ♠ A, and ruff a third round of diamonds on the board. Safety dictates that trump be pulled first. The ♠ A should be forced next, and the diamond ruff is last.

The opening lead and play to Trick 2 indicate that West started with four cards in the diamond suit, while East began with three. Declarer can remove East's diamond guard and isolate the diamond menace against West by trumping a third round of the suit in dummy. However, this play must be made after the ♠ A has been forced. If not, a fourth round of diamonds will be played by the defense when they gain the lead with the ♠ A, and the single menace disappears.

This is how the play should go starting with trick 3. Trump is drawn in three rounds and the ♠ A is driven out by playing the ♠ K. West's return, probably the ♠ J, is taken in the closed hand and a diamond is trumped in dummy. A club to South's ♣ A brings about this four-card ending.

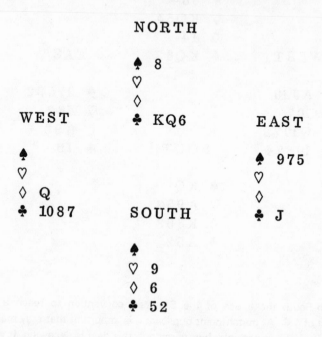

NORTH

♠ 8
♡
◇
♣ KQ6

WEST

♠
♡
◇ Q
♣ 1087

EAST

♠ 975
♡
◇
♣ J

SOUTH

♠
♡ 9
◇ 6
♣ 52

The hand has been reduced to the First Entry Form (Automatic). If either opponent began the hand with four or more cards in both minor suits, he will be Squeezed. It is just this type of hand the bridge expert looks for in tournament play. He knows the cards will lie favorably only a small percentage of the time, but when they do, he will reap a bushel of match-points. The important point, however, is that no other line of play need be sacrificed in order to try for this squeeze.

## NORTH

♠ A5
♡ KQJ10
◊ 1093
♣ Q942

## SOUTH

♠ Q8
♡ 9865432
◊ A84
♣ A

**The Auction:**

| WEST | NORTH | EAST | SOUTH |
|------|-------|------|-------|
| 1 ♠  | Dbl.  | 2 ♠  | 4 ♡   |
| Pass | Pass  | Pass |       |

**Opening Lead:** ◊ Q

**Trick 1:** ◊Q-3-7 ?

## Plan your play.

NORTH

♠ A 5
♡ K Q J 10
♢ 10 9 3
♣ Q 9 4 2

WEST                                                    EAST

♠ K J 10 9 3                                        ♠ 7 6 4 2
♡ A                                                        ♡ 7
♢ Q J 6                                                  ♢ K 7 5 2
♣ K 10 7 5          SOUTH          ♣ J 8 6 3

♠ Q 8
♡ 9 8 6 5 4 3 2
♢ A 8 4
♣ A

South moves directly to a heart game in response to his partner's take-out double.

Your first course of action when declaring any hand, and particularly before playing to Trick 1, should be to count your winners. On this particular deal there are six heart tricks plus three side Aces for a total of nine winners, one trick short of your contract. You must also take stock of the opponents' assets and where they are likely to lie.

Your partnership owns a total of 22 high card points. This leaves the enemy in possession of 18 hcp. The opening lead suggests the location of the ♦ K as being with East. From the 15 hcp remaining it is almost impossible to construct an opening bid for West that does not contain both black Kings. That makes LHO a prime target for a squeeze.

Declarer cannot afford to win either of the first two diamond tricks. To do so would allow East to gain the lead with the ♦ K. Once on lead, your RHO is sure to lead a spade. This play would destroy your split threat and any chance of actuating a squeeze against West.

LHO gives maximum defense by cashing the ♥ A to avoid any possibility of an End-Play before continuing with his third diamond. Declarer wins Trick 4 with the ♦ A and checks out the four conditions of the BLUE Law for a club-spade squeeze against West. Everything seems to be in good working order.

It is time to set the squeeze machine in motion, but don't overlook any normal line of play that might make the hand without resorting to a squeeze. Possibly the ♣ K lies doubleton or third in the hand to your left. You should play for this contingency as part of your count-down.

Start by cashing the ♣ A and get it out of the way. Cross to dummy in hearts and trump a small club. Cash the remaining high hearts in dummy and trump the last small club. If the ♣ K has not appeared, go on with your Squeeze. The last three cards look like this.

```
                      NORTH
                      ♠ A 5
                      ♡
                      ◇
       WEST           ♣ Q           EAST
       ♠ KJ                         ♠ 76
       ♡                            ♡
       ◇                            ◇
       ♣ K          SOUTH           ♣ J
                      ♠ Q8
                      ♡ 9
                      ◇
                      ♣
```

Our squeeze is the Third Entry Form (Positional) against West. The only card to watch for is the ♣ K. If West has not released the ♣ K, North's ♣ Q becomes worthless and is discarded on the squeeze trick.

LHO has been squeezed.

## The Auction:

| NORTH | SOUTH | WEST | NORTH | EAST |
|-------|-------|------|-------|------|
| ♠ K652 | 1 ♡ | 1 ♠ | Dbl.* | Rdbl.** |
| ♡ A4 | Pass | 2 ◊ | Dbl. | Rdbl. |
| ◊ K1052 | 3 ◊ | Dbl. | Rdbl.*** | Pass |
| ♣ 643 | 4 ♡ | Pass | Pass | Pass |

|       |                              |
|-------|------------------------------|
|       | * Cooperative Business Dbl. |
| SOUTH | ** S.O.S. Redouble.          |
|       | *** A stopper for N.T.       |

♠ A83
♡ KQ10852    Opening Lead: ♠ Q
◊
♣ A952

Trick 1: ♠Q-2-7-A
Trick 2: ♡2-3-A-J
Trick 3: ♡4-K-6 East ◊3
Trick 4: ?

Plan your play.

NORTH

♠ K652
♡ A4
◇ K1052
♣ 643

WEST

♠ QJ1094
♡ 9763
◇ AQ6
♣ 10

EAST

♠ 7
♡ J
◇ J98743
♣ KQJ87

SOUTH

♠ A83
♡ KQ10852
◇
♣ A952

By Trick 3 declarer has gathered the following information about the West hand. He should have a five-card spade suit for his overcall. We also know he has four hearts. In addition he indicated a preference for diamonds by bidding 2 ◆ in response to the SOS redouble. With equal length in the minors he would have bid 1 NT. If ever there was a man with a singleton or void in clubs, West is it.

After pulling trump we must try to set up a squeeze against West. This can be done using spades as a double menace and the ◆ K as a single menace, providing the ◆ A was part of the values LHO used for his original overcall. But first we must rectify the count. In doing so West cannot be allowed to gain the lead, for he is sure to play another spade and deprive us of condition E. LHO can be kept out of the lead by cashing the ♣ A and leading a club to East. He cannot break our squeeze. His best play is to win his three club tricks and exit with a diamond. If he leads a diamond before taking all three clubs, South pitches a club. West wins the ◆ A, but the ◆ K becomes our tenth trick. Here is the ending after East wins his third club.

### NORTH

♠ K6
♡
◊ K10
♣

| WEST | | EAST |
|---|---|---|
| ♠ J10 | | ♠ |
| ♡ | | ♡ |
| ◊ AQ | | ◊ J98 |
| ♣ | | ♣ 8 |

### SOUTH

♠ 83
♡ 85
◊
♣

East can play either minor. South ruffs as West and North both toss diamonds. The play of the last heart from the closed hand squeezes West.

**NORTH**

♠ A953
♡ Q43
◇ K10982
♣ 4

**SOUTH**

♠ KQ2
♡ J42
◇ A65
♣ AK63

The Auction:

| SOUTH | WEST | NORTH | EAST |
|-------|------|-------|------|
| 1 N.T. | Pass | 2 ♣ | Pass |
| 2 ◇ | Pass | 3 N.T. | Pass |
| Pass | Pass | | |

Opening Lead: ♡ 7

Trick 1: ♡7-3-10-J
Trick 2: ?

**Plan your play.**

### NORTH

♠ A 9 5 3
♡ Q 4 3
◊ K 10 9 8 2
♣ 4

WEST

♠ 10 6
♡ A K 9 7 6
◊ J 7
♣ 10 9 8 5

EAST

♠ J 8 7 4
♡ 10 8
◊ Q 4 3
♣ Q J 7 2

### SOUTH

♠ K Q 2
♡ J 5 2
◊ A 6 5
♣ A K 6 3

The philosophy of "let's not lose a trick" will lose this hand. The untutored declarer plays spades first, and when they fail to split three-three he tries the ♦ A K in hopes of finding the ♦ Q J doubleton. When this also fails he had better take the ♣ A K or he may not get both of them. His maximum result is down one on a hand that cannot be beaten if played properly.

When playing any hand at 3 NT, you must not only arrange to take nine winners for yourself, but you must also prevent the enemy from winning five tricks on defense. The best way to keep the opposition from winning five tricks is to graciously surrender four. In other words, apply the theory of maximum pressure by rectifying the count.

This deal will produce nine winners by giving up a diamond trick if the suit splits three-two or if they split four-one and a diamond honor is singleton. However, the moment either defender gains the lead he will play hearts. The opening lead may have been made from a five-card holding, in which case the contract will be defeated.

If the spade suit divides evenly there is no problem, but if it does not there is the possibility of a spade-diamond squeeze against East. This requires that you bring condition L into line. If you can't rectify the count for yourself, let your opponent's do it for you. Lead hearts? If the suit divides four-three, your opponents can take only three defensive tricks. When you regain the lead, a diamond can be given up to make the hand. If the heart suit splits five-two, the defense takes four tricks and L is in order for your squeeze. Only if LHO refuses to cash all of his winners can the squeeze be prevented, but it is safe to now give up a diamond trick to East. The heart communication has been broken and West cannot take the setting trick. Here is the position after West has taken his four heart winners.

```
                    NORTH
                    ♠ A 9 5 3
                    ♡
                    ◊ K 10 9 8
     WEST           ♣              EAST
     ♠ 10 6                        ♠ J 8 7 4
     ♡                             ♡
     ◊ J 7                         ◊ Q 4 3
     ♣ 10 9 8 5     SOUTH          ♣ Q
                    ♠ K Q 2
                    ♡
                    ◊ A 6 5
                    ♣ A K
```

West can exit safely in either black suit. He is most likely to choose clubs. South takes the trick as the ♦ 8 is tossed from the dummy. the ♦ K and ♦ A are played leaving this end position.

## NORTH

♠ A 9 5 3
♡
◊ 10
♣

## WEST

♠ 10 6
♡
◊
♣ 9 8 6

## EAST

♠ J 8 7 4
♡
◊ Q
♣

## SOUTH

♠ K Q 2
♡
◊ 6
♣ K

South leads the ♣ K and throws the ◊ 10 from dummy. The ◊ 6 in his own hand will serve equally well as the single menace.

East is squeezed.

## The Auction:

**NORTH**

♠ 8532
♡ J6
◊ AK5
♣ A982

| SOUTH | WEST | NORTH | EAST |
|-------|------|-------|------|
| 1 ♠ | 2 N.T.* | Dbl. | Pass |
| Pass | 3 ♣ | Dbl. | Pass |
| 4 ♠ | Pass | 4 N.T. | Pass |
| 5 ◊ | Pass | 6 ♠ | Pass |
| Pass | Pass | | |

**SOUTH**

♠ KQJ106
♡ AKQ
◊ 963
♣ KQ

\* Unusual N.T. for minors.

Opening Lead: ◊ Q

Trick 1: ◊Q-A-4-3
Trick 2: ♠2-4-K West ♣3
Trick 3: ?

Plan your play.

### NORTH

♠ 8532
♡ J6
◇ AK5
♣ A982

WEST | EAST

♠
♡ 83
◇ QJ1087
♣ J107543

♠ A974
♡ 1097542
◇ 42
♣ 6

### SOUTH

♠ KQJ106
♡ AKQ
◇ 963
♣ KQ

How often have you watched a player lose his composure at the table when the forces of adverse distribution play their dirty little tricks? On this deal, declarer literally went to pieces. When trump broke badly he became upset, began throwing cards, and eventually conceded down one on a hand that actually could have been made.

West led the ♦ Q which was won in dummy. A spade to the King revealed the four-zero trump break and the fact that the ♠ 8 would not be available as a much-needed entry to the board. East won the spade continuation with the ♠ A and continued diamonds. This removed a vital entry from dummy.

In view of the bidding declarer cannot play out the ♠ K Q in advance or East will trump in, but there should be a minor suit squeeze against West. East's diamond return is taken in dummy and two more rounds of spades are played removing all of East's trump. Three rounds of high hearts follow leaving this four-card ending.

# THE SIMPLE SQUEEZE IN BRIDGE

### NORTH

♠
♡
◊ 5
♣ A 9 8

**WEST**

♠
♡
◊ J
♣ J 10 7

**EAST**

♠
♡ 10 9 7
◊
♣ 6

**SOUTH**

♠ 6
♡
◊ 9
♣ K Q

Dummy's ◆ 5 is thrown on the play of the ♠ 6 from the closed hand.
West is squeezed.

A club discard allows South to win the ♣ K and overtake the ♣ Q as an
entry to dummy while a diamond discard establishes declarers ◆ 9.

## Chapter V

# Advanced Squeeze Development

Not every squeeze is as clear cut and easy to recognize as the examples and problem hands to which you have been exposed thus far. In fact, some of the examples shown in this chapter are not squeezes at all. However, they do illustrate how squeeze techniques may be used to accomplish a different end. In this chapter you will also find several advanced squeeze situations including the FOURTH ENTRY FORM, previously mentioned in Chapter I.

### Complex Squeeze Situations

The intricacies of who is to be subjected to your squeeze and exactly what threats are available to use against them often lie hidden in a welter of extraneous card combinations. As declarer, it is your task to sort out all threat possibilities and apply the BLUE Law to each. You may find that one particular line of play offers more than one squeeze possibility against the same defender, or that you are able to operate two squeezes simultaneously, one against each opponent. Selecting your squeeze victim will not always be an easy affair. The conditions of BLUE may be obscured by a complexity of suit arrangements and entry forms. You must choose not only the squeeze or squeezes which have the best possibility of existing but which also have the greatest probability of succeeding.

NORTH

♠ K852
♡ J864
◇ K
♣ AK83

WEST                                 EAST

♠ J7                                 ♠ Q94
♡ 1073                               ♡ 9
◇ 109764                             ◇ AQ52
♣ J65          SOUTH                 ♣ Q10972

♠ A1063
♡ AKQ52
◇ J83
♣ 4

The Auction:

| NORTH | EAST | SOUTH | EAST |
|-------|------|-------|------|
| 1 ♣ | Pass | 1 ♡ | Pass |
| 2 ♡ | Pass | 2 ♠ | Pass |
| 3 ♠ | Pass | 4 N.T. | Pass |
| 5 ◇ | Dbl. | Pass* | Pass |
| 6 ♡ | Pass | Pass | Pass |

* Are there two Diamond losers?

Opening Lead: ◇ 10

123

A declarer in search of a squeeze may sometimes be compared to a thirsty man on a desert. He looks and looks for a squeeze, but each time he thinks he has found one it turns out to be a mirage.

At first sight there seems to be a squeeze possibility here using the obvious ♦ J as a single menace and the spade suit as a double or compound menace. You can try this in two ways. If you trump a diamond on the board and cash the ♣ A K before you run your hearts you will come to ten tricks. You may also cash the ♣ A K and ruff out two small clubs from the table in a dummy reversal. This will also give you a total of ten tricks, but neither play will bring you to an eleven winner-one loser situation needed to satisfy Condition L.

The only way to develop eleven winners and give yourself a chance for a squeeze is to trump both diamonds on the board, but his leaves you without a single menace. Your only hope, and it is a slim one, is to find one opponent in possession of five clubs and three or more spades.

East wins the ♦ A and returns the ♥ 9. Through careful play, declarer should be able to reduce the hand to this six-card ending.

NORTH

♠ K852
♡
♦
♣ 83

WEST

♠ J7
♡ 10
♦ 97
♣ J

EAST

♠ Q94
♡
♦
♣ Q109

SOUTH

♠ A106
♡ Q52
♦
♣

# THE SIMPLE SQUEEZE IN BRIDGE

A club is played from the North hand and ruffed by South. This isolates the club menace against East. The ♥ Q removes West's last trump as a spade is tossed from Dummy. South's last heart administers the club-spade squeeze to East as another spade is pitched from the open hand.

<pre>
                    NORTH

                  ♠ QJ
                  ♡ A843
                  ◊ A642
        WEST      ♣ KQJ        EAST

      ♠ 873                  ♠ 52
      ♡ QJ7                  ♡ 92
      ◊ KQJ1083             ◊ 975
      ♣ 8           SOUTH    ♣ 976432

                  ♠ AK10964
                  ♡ K1065
                  ◊
                  ♣ A105
</pre>

## The Auction:

| WEST | NORTH | EAST | SOUTH |
|------|-------|------|-------|
| 2 ◊* | Dbl.** | 7 ◊ | 7 ♠ |
| Pass | Pass | Pass | |

* Weak 2 Bid.
** Weiss Dbl. = 1 N.T. Opening Bid.

Opening Lead: ◊ K

The game is match-point duplicate where a profitable save can be worth much more than at rubber bridge. By partnership agreement East knows his partner cannot have two Aces and open the bidding with a Weak 2 Bid. His drastic pre-emptive bid of 7 ♦ on a hand with no defensive value is meant as a premature save. North-South are, thereby, deprived of any bidding room to investigate the slam potential of their combined hands. South is forced to bid 7 ♠ blindly and offer up a short prayer.

There are three ways this contract can be made, and they all involve a favorable lie of cards in the heart suit. West could have a singleton ♥ Q or ♥ J. The ♥ A in dummy is then cashed and a finesse taken against East's remaining honor. Either opponent could hold a doubleton ♥ Q J in which case they would fall beneath the ♥ A K. LHO could hold the heart length plus six or more diamonds and be subjected to a squeeze. Declarer must play out the hand so as to give himself all three possibilities, but also he must be able to tell which one, if any, is succeeding.

Declarer immediately begins the process of isolating the diamond menace against West by ruffing the opening lead in the closed hand. He extracts trump in three rounds noting that West held three pieces. A club is played to the North hand followed by the ♦ A and a small diamond. A small heart from South is discarded on the ♦ A and the small diamond is ruffed. If West started with a six-card diamond suit as he should have, the remaining card on the board becomes a single threat against him.

To complete his count of the opponent's distribution declarer plays off his two remaining clubs. West fails to follow. He started with a singleton. LHO is known to have begun this hand with three spades, a singleton club, and five or six diamonds. There is no way he can have a singleton Heart honor or a doubleton ♥ Q J. Our only remaining hope is the squeeze. If West opened a Weak 2 Bid with five diamonds and four hearts, East still has a diamond and our Squeeze is going to fail for lack of B. However, it is much more likely that the opponent to our left had six diamonds and three hearts in which case our play is going to succeed.

Declarer proceeds with the count down by running his remaining trump winners. This is the squeeze ending as the last spade is being played.

# THE SIMPLE SQUEEZE IN BRIDGE

## NORTH

♠
♡ A 8 4
◇ 6
♣

**WEST**

♠
♡ Q J 7
◇ Q
♣

**EAST**

♠
♡ 9 2
◇
♣ 9 7

## SOUTH

♠ 6
♡ K 10 6
◇
♣

As you can see, the lead of South's ♠ 6 subjects West to a squeeze.

                            NORTH

                        ♠ 42
                        ♡ K1052
                        ◊ KJ53
        WEST            ♣ K43            EAST

    ♠ A98753                             ♠ J10
    ♡ 84                                 ♡ 76
    ◊ 1098                               ◊ Q762
    ♣ J8            SOUTH                ♣ Q9752

                        ♠ KQ6
                        ♡ AQJ93
                        ◊ A4
                        ♣ A106

The Auction:

    NORTH       EAST        SOUTH       WEST

    Pass        Pass        1 ♡         Pass
    3 ♡         Pass        6 ♡         Pass
    Pass        Pass

Opening Lead: ◊ 10

# THE SIMPLE SQUEEZE IN BRIDGE

There seem to be only eleven tricks on this hand: five hearts, two diamonds, and two clubs, plus a spade and a spade ruff. There are three ways to develop a twelfth trick. One, the ♣ Q J may be doubleton; two, the ♠ A may be to the right; or three, an extra winner may be promoted in the diamond suit.

South takes the first step by refusing the diamond finesse. He judges that West has not elected to lead the ♦ 10 from a holding of ♦ Q 10 9 in defense of a slam contract; therefore, the ♦ A is taken in the closed hand. Trumps are drawn in two rounds ending in dummy and a spade is led. The ♠ K loses to LHO's ♠ A. West continues the ♦ 9. The ♦ K is won on the board and a small diamond is ruffed trying to drop the ♦ Q from the East hand. When this play fails our slam seems doomed. The ♠ Q is led and a small spade is ruffed in the North hand. East pitches a club. Wait a minute! East has only two spades. If he holds the ♦ Q plus doubletons in both majors, he is left with five clubs. This means West has only a doubleton club and cannot protect the suit. East can be caught in a squeeze. Here is our present position with the lead on the board.

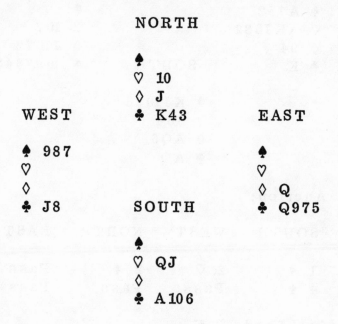

```
                    NORTH
                    ♠
                    ♡  10
                    ◊  J
                    ♣  K43
     WEST                              EAST
     ♠  987                            ♠
     ♡                                 ♡
     ◊                                 ◊  Q
     ♣  J8          SOUTH              ♣  Q975
                    ♠
                    ♡  QJ
                    ◊
                    ♣  A106
```

129

A heart is used to re-enter the South hand. East has an Idle club for this trick, but on the second Heart a club is thrown from the open hand and East is squeezed.

## The Count Squeeze

The *Count* squeeze or *Show-up* squeeze, as it is more often called, is the use of squeeze procedures to avoid the taking of a finesse. There are two variations to the play.

```
                        NORTH

                    ♠ Q643
                    ♡ Q9
                    ◊ K853
                    ♣ J85
        WEST                        EAST

    ♠ A752                     ♠
    ♡ AKJ532                   ♡ 107
    ◊ 94                       ◊ J1072
    ♣ K          SOUTH         ♣ 10976432

                    ♠ KJ1098
                    ♡ 864
                    ◊ AQ6
                    ♣ AQ
```

The Auction:

| SOUTH | WEST | NORTH | EAST |
|-------|------|-------|------|
| 1 ♠   | 2 ♡  | 2 ♠   | Pass |
| 4 ♠   | Pass | Pass  | Pass |

Opening Lead: ♡ K

# THE SIMPLE SQUEEZE IN BRIDGE

South bids a spade game that seems to have two chances to make. Either the diamond suit must divide evenly and provide a place to discard the ♣ Q, or the club finesse must be successful. However, there is one additional possibility. If four or more diamonds and the ♣ K lie in the same hand we also have a squeeze.

West puts up a stubborn defense. He wins the first two heart tricks with the ♥ A K, and, upon seeing his partner's high-low signal, he continues the suit. The third heart is trumped in dummy with the ♠ Q as East discards a club. East fails to follow suit for the second time when a trump is played from the North hand. This places ten major suit cards with the LHO and eleven cards in the minors to our right.

There is virtually no chance that the diamond suit will divide favorably; however, the count of the hand to date tells us that East is the only opponent that can possibly hold the diamond length. The hand should be played with this in mind.

West offers the best possible defense by refusing the ♠ A until the third round when there is no longer any trump in dummy. He now returns a heart in an attempt to use up declarer's trump holding.

Throughout the play of this hand we should be watching for diamond discards. The fourth diamond in dummy will eventually become our single menace. We hope to have East squeezed between the diamond single menace and the double menace of the ♣ A Q. This is our present situation.

### NORTH

♠  
♡  
◊ K853  
♣ J8  

### WEST

♠ 7  
♡ 53  
◊ 94  
♣ K  

### EAST

♠  
♡  
◊ J 10 7 2  
♣ 10 9  

### SOUTH

♠ 9  
♡  
◊ A Q 6  
♣ A Q  

Our ♠ 9 takes West's last trump. It is also our squeeze card if East is Busy in both diamonds and clubs. When the play of three top diamonds reveals the fact that the suit does not split three-three, a club is led from the open hand. East plays small. The other card in East's hand is known to be the outstanding diamond; therefore, the club finesse cannot succeed. Declarer goes up with the ♣ A and is rewarded for his efforts by dropping the singleton ♣ K off side.

In the truest sense of the word no squeeze has occurred. East never did have Busy cards in two suits. Yet, unless declarer "peeked" at West's hand, the loss of no club tricks could only be worked out by employing squeeze techniques.

In the example you have just seen the finessing tenace was in the upper hand, behind the squeeze victim. A show-up squeeze may also occur with the tenace in the lower hand.

NORTH

♠ KJ83
♡ 1093
◊ A964
♣ AQ

WEST

♠ 95
♡ KJ842
◊ 10
♣ 108732

EAST

♠ Q1072
♡ Q76
◊ QJ7
♣ 954

SOUTH

♠ A64
♡ A5
◊ K8532
♣ KJ6

The Auction:

| SOUTH | WEST | NORTH | EAST |
|-------|------|-------|------|
| 1 ◊ | Pass | 1 ♠ | Pass |
| 1 N.T. | Pass | 3 ◊ | Pass |
| 3 ♡ | Pass | 3 N.T. | Pass |
| Pass | Pass | | |

Opening Lead: ♡ 4

# THE SIMPLE SQUEEZE IN BRIDGE

In this deal as in any other that may or may not contain a squeeze, Declarer starts his play in a perfectly normal manner. Hearts are held up one round and the diamond suit is played next, first the ♦ K and then the ♦ A in dummy. Only when diamonds fail to divide evenly do we look elsewhere for our game-fulfilling ninth trick. A long suit winner cannot be established in diamonds without giving up the lead. The defense will then take this diamond plus four hearts for down one. A spade finesse offers another possibility for our ninth winner. But must this all-or-nothing play be made so early in the hand? Declarer would do well to remember the theory of maximum pressure. Your best course of action is to give the lead back to the opposition and postpone any decision in the spade suit until a later date. Lead the ♥ 10 and discard a Spade from the South hand. As the player to your left cashes two more hearts, diamonds are thrown from both North and South. East parts with a spade and a club to arrive at this 5 card end position.

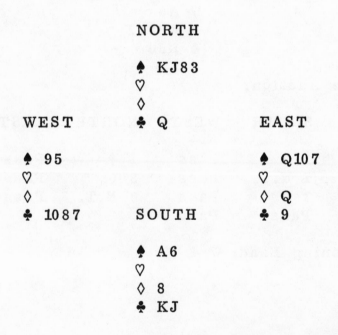

```
                    NORTH

                ♠ KJ83
                ♡
                ◊
WEST            ♣ Q          EAST

♠ 95                         ♠ Q10 7
♡                            ♡
◊                            ◊ Q
♣ 1087          SOUTH        ♣ 9

                ♠ A6
                ♡
                ◊ 8
                ♣ KJ
```

134

LHO exits with either black suit. Since it makes no difference which suit, let's say he leads clubs. South wins and cashes his last high club. When East fails to follow suit, his distributional pattern is completely exposed. He started with three hearts, three diamonds, and three clubs. This means he began the hand with four spades and his partner with two spades. Assume for the moment that the ♦ Q is still missing and the ♦ 8 has not become a winner. Declarer plays the ♠ A followed by the ♠ 6. When West fails to show up with the ♠ Q on the second play of the suit he cannot have the card. We have seen both of his spades. The play of dummy's ♠ K drops East's ♠ Q. This time East, the hand behind the spade tenace, was legitimately squeezed in diamonds and spades.

Take a moment to consider what happens if West refuses to take his fifth heart in an effort to keep his partner from being squeezed. Here is the end position.

NORTH

♠ KJ83
♡
◊ 9
♣ Q

WEST

♠ 95
♡ 8
◊
♣ 1087

EAST

♠ Q107
♡
◊ Q
♣ 95

SOUTH

♠ A6
♡
◊ 85
♣ KJ

Again West gets out with a Club. Declarer wins the club and simply leads a diamond to establish his ninth trick. West clearly has no entry to cash his last heart.

## Combination Squeeze Situations

It is possible to develop more than one single squeeze situation on the same hand. When there is one single squeeze possibility against each opponent, the position is known as an *Alternative Squeeze*. There is no name that I know of for a situation involving two single squeeze possibilities against the same opponent. We will, therefore, give it a name and call it a *Dual Squeeze*.

## The Alternative Squeeze

The alternative squeeze, which is sometimes called the Either-Or Squeeze is a close relative to the double squeeze; a subject that will not be taken up in this book. The situation evolves when one opponent is found to be Busy in one suit while his partner is known to be Busy in another. This establishes a single menace against each. One opponent controls a third suit in which a double menace or compound menace exists, but the defender in control is unknown. The only answer is to run a single squeeze against each of them between the suit they are known to have plus the third suit in which control may lie with either opponent.

```
                    NORTH

                  ♠ Q6
                  ♡ Q4
                  ◊ K8542
      WEST        ♣ AQJ4        EAST

   ♠ ?8754                    ♠ ?932
   ♡ 9                        ♡ 108752
   ◊ J1097                    ◊ 3
   ♣ 972        SOUTH         ♣ 653

                  ♠ AJ
                  ♡ AKJ63
                  ◊ AQ6
                  ♣ K108
```

## The Auction:

| SOUTH | WEST | NORTH | EAST |
|-------|------|-------|------|
| 2 ♡ | Pass | 3 ◊ | Pass |
| 3 N.T. | Pass | 4 ♣ | Pass |
| 4 ◊ | Pass | 4 N.T. | Pass |
| 5 ♠ | Pass | 5 N.T. | Pass |
| 6 ♡ | Pass | 7 N.T. | Pass |
| Pass | Pass | | |

Opening Lead: ◊ J

# THE SIMPLE SQUEEZE IN BRIDGE

When dummy hits the table South thinks his Grand Slam is a sure thing. If both the heart suit and the diamond suit run, there are no less than fifteen winners to be had. Declarer wins the ♦ A and plays the ♦ Q. When East shows out by pitching the ♣ 3, the hand begins to turn sour. The ♥ Q followed by the ♥ A completes the ugly picture. We now have only twelve sure winners. The hand seems to hinge on a spade finesse, or does it?

What are our squeeze possibilities? If West has the ♠ K, he is subject to a First Entry Form (Automatic) squeeze between a small diamond in the North hand for a single menace and a double threat in spades. If East holds the ♠ K, in addition to being finessable he can be caught in a squeeze using a small heart in the closed hand for a single threat and spades as a double menace, or show-up suit.

Which squeeze should we play for? The answer is simple, both. First cash the Heart winners in the South hand. A small Diamond and the ♠ 6 are eliminated from Dummy. The remaining high diamond is played from North, and the club suit is run. Here is our position before dummy's last club is played.

```
                    NORTH
                    ♠  Q
                    ♡
                    ◊  8
                    ♣  J
     WEST                          EAST
     ♠  ?8                         ♠  ?9
     ♡                             ♡  10
     ◊  10                         ◊
     ♣                   SOUTH     ♣
                    ♠  A J
                    ♡  6
                    ◊
                    ♣
```

The ♣ J is led from the table. East is squeezed positionally in spades and hearts. He must hold the heart and hope spades can be protected by his partner. After East discards the ♠ 9 the ♥ 6 becomes an Idle card and serves as a free discard from the South hand. West is now squeezed in diamonds and spades. Either discard is fatal.

By this time I am sure you have noticed that the location of the ♠ K and the ♠ 10 have been obscured by question marks. This is done to dramatize the point that the position of the ♠ K is immaterial to the success or failure of your contract. One of your opponents has been the victim of a show-up squeeze. Who really had the ♠ K you ask? It was with West. Assuming the same lead, the Q J of spades were unnecessary to fulfilling our contract—the helpless E-W defenders were forced to relinquish control to protect their respective menaces.

### NORTH

♠ K4
♡ AK93
◊ KQ
♣ A8542

### WEST

♠ 7
♡ 10764
◊ 9873
♣ K1073

### EAST

♠ A9853
♡ J52
◊ 1052
♣ J9

### SOUTH

♠ QJ1062
♡ Q8
◊ AJ64
♣ Q6

## The Auction:

| SOUTH | WEST | NORTH | EAST |
|-------|------|-------|------|
| 1 ♠ | Pass | 2 ♣ | Pass |
| 2 ◊ | Pass | 2 ♡ | Pass |
| 2 N.T. | Pass | 4 N.T. | Pass |
| 5 ◊ | Pass | 6 N.T. | Pass |
| Pass | Pass | | |

## Opening Lead: ◊ 9

# THE SIMPLE SQUEEZE IN BRIDGE

South's questionable opening bid leads to a small slam at No Trump being played from his own hand. Trick 1 is won in dummy and the ♠ K is played. East wins and continues a spade. The contract is assured if West follows suit. When he throws a club, declarer starts looking for a possible squeeze.

Our fifth spade is a single menace against East. He may also hold the ♣ K. No squeeze can be developed here. Declarer's club holding is a split threat and can only be used in the Third Entry Form. All Third Entry Form squeezes are positional and require that the upper hand contain the single menace and the split threat entry card. The club honors are positioned improperly for this play to work.

If East holds four or more hearts to go with his Busy spades, he can be squeezed, but is this the only possibility available to us? Could West be a suitable victim? Three rounds of hearts can be played leaving the last one in dummy as a single threat against West but we have no entry back to the closed hand to run a Third Entry Form (Positional) squeeze against West. Also, if East is to be squeezed, playing hearts removes E.

The answer to our problem is to unblock the ♣ A. It must be cleared from dummy to give us the ♣ Q as a single menace to count out a club-heart squeeze against the hand to our left. The spade-heart squeeze will not operate against the hand to our right unless the ♣ A is played early. The last diamond honor in the open hand is cleared before re-entering the south hand with the ♥ Q for the count down. The high spades and diamonds are played from the closed hand. This is our position before the last diamond is led.

NORTH

♠
♡ A K 9
♢
♣ 8

WEST                EAST

♠                              ♠ 9
♡ 10 7 6                   ♡ J 5
♢                              ♢
♣ K     SOUTH     ♣ J

♠ 6
♡ 8
♢ J
♣ Q

East is known to hold the ranking spade. We hope West has the ♣ K. If this is so, the play of our last diamond has to squeeze the defender who started with four or more hearts, in this case West.

Notice the importance of clearing the ♣ A from dummy before the count down. If West is our victim we have an easily countable hand by watching for the ♣ K. If East is to be squeezed and the ♣ A is not cashed, our squeeze fails. This would be the end position if East had started with four hearts and the ♣ A were still in dummy.

<pre>
                    NORTH
                    ♠
                    ♡  A K 9
                    ◊
    WEST            ♣  A 8            EAST

    ♠                                ♠  9
    ♡  10 7                          ♡  J 5 4
    ◊  8                             ◊
    ♣  K 10         SOUTH            ♣  J

                    ♠  6
                    ♡  8
                    ◊  J
                    ♣  Q 6
</pre>

East is left with an Idle card, the ♣ J, and avoids our squeeze by using it as a free discard on the ♦ J, our squeeze card.

## The Dual Squeeze

It is possible to find one opponent Busy in a double menace suit with a choice of more than one single menace to use to complete our squeeze requirements. In effect we evolve two single squeeze possibilities against the same opponent.

## The Squeeze Without the Count

You have been told up until now that the BLUE law is infallible, and that each of the four conditions and each of the four entry forms is absolute, allowing for no variation. This is not quite so. Given just the right circumstnaces condition L can fail to be in proper order.

A squeeze without the count, or *ducking squeeze* occurs when declarer executes his squeeze with a loser count that is greater than one. The lead is given to a defender after the squeeze has taken place to rectify the count.

```
                    NORTH

                  ♠ A93
                  ♡ AQ94
                  ◊ 8652
       WEST       ♣ AJ            EAST

    ♠ 7                         ♠ 542
    ♡ 106                       ♡ J8752
    ◊ KQJ104                    ◊ 7
    ♣ KQ865        SOUTH        ♣ 10732

                  ♠ KQJ1086
                  ♡ K3
                  ◊ A93
                  ♣ 94
```

The Auction:

| SOUTH | WEST | NORTH | EAST |
|-------|------|-------|------|
| 1 ♠ | 2 N.T.* | Dbl. | 3 ♣ |
| 4 ♠ | Pass | 4 N.T. | Pass |
| 5 ◊ | Pass | 5 N.T. | Pass |
| 6 ♡ | Pass | 6 ♠ | Pass |
| Pass | Pass | | |

\* Unusual N.T. for the minors.

Opening Lead: ◊ K

If the hand were played at No Trump instead of a suit contract, declarer would have no problem. He would duck the opening diamond lead to rectify the count and develop a First Entry Form squeeze against West using the minor suits.

With spades as trump the ♦ K cannot be allowed to win. East's hot breath can be heard as he stands waiting in the wings to trump the diamond continuation. We will have to win this trick and worry about how to rectify the count at some later date.

The ♦ A is won and trump is drawn in three rounds. West releases one card from each of his five-card minors. Next comes four rounds of hearts. South pitches a diamond on the third round and ruffs the fourth. West throws two clubs. This is our current situation.

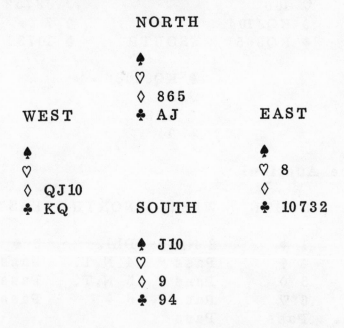

```
                    NORTH
                    ♠
                    ♡
                    ◊ 8 6 5
     WEST           ♣ A J          EAST

     ♠                              ♠
     ♡                              ♡ 8
     ◊ Q J 10                       ◊
     ♣ K Q          SOUTH           ♣ 10 7 3 2
                    ♠ J 10
                    ♡
                    ◊ 9
                    ♣ 9 4
```

The two remaining spades are played. West is caught in a Third Entry Form (Positional) squeeze, but with a loser count of two. He can discard a diamond on the first Spade, but the second one actuates the squeeze. If West discards a club, the results are obvious; therefore, he must play a diamond. After he does, the ♣ J becomes worthless and is eliminated from the North hand. The play of a diamond gives LHO the lead and simultaneously rectifies the count. His forced club return to dummy accounts for the last two tricks.

NORTH

♠ 65432
♡ AK4
◊ Q
♣ A853

WEST

♠ QJ1087
♡ Q10973
◊ A8
♣ J

EAST

♠
♡ J8
◊ 97642
♣ Q109742

SOUTH

♠ AK9
♡ 652
◊ KJ1053
♣ K6

The Auction:

| SOUTH | WEST | NORTH | EAST |
|-------|------|-------|------|
| 1 ◊ | 2 ◊* | 2 ♠ | Pass |
| 2 N.T. | Pass | 3 ♣ | Pass |
| 3 ♠ | Pass | 4 ♠ | Pass |
| Pass | Dbl. | 4 N.T. | Pass |
| Pass | Dbl. | Pass | Pass |
| Pass | | | |

* Michaels Cue-Bid - 6-11 hcp
  Min. five-four in majors.

Opening Lead: ♠ Q

147

South becomes declarer at a contract of 4 NT when North has second thoughts about playing 4 ♠ doubled.

The ♠ Q opening lead is taken in the closed hand and a diamond is played toward dummy's ♦ Q. West ducks. The Michael's Cue-Bid marks LHO with a minimum of five-four distribution in the majors. We know about the five spades, but what is the rest of his distributional pattern? If he has three diamonds we have ten winners. If he has three diamonds and five hearts, East is defenseless in the heart suit and West can be squeezed for an overtrick. As the distribution actually is, we have an extremely rare *squeeze without the count* based upon a loser count of three. This end position is also known as a double ducking squeeze, and you will soon see why.

The ♣ A is cashed from dummy and a small one is returned to South's ♣ K. The ♦ K forces West's ♦ A. He plays another high spade. South takes the ♠ K and loads another high Diamond. West shows out pitching a heart. We now know his complete distribution. Here is our position with 7 cards remaining.

NORTH

♠ 654
♡ AK4
◊
♣

WEST

♠ 1087
♡ Q10 9
◊
♣

EAST

♠
♡ J8
◊ 97
♣ Q10

SOUTH

♠ 9
♡ 652
◊ 105
♣

South plays the ♦ 10 and West is squeezed. Even though we have only three winners out of the last six tricks, leaving an outstanding loser count of three, the squeeze is effective. If West throws a heart the results are plain to see. He must, therefore, release a spade. The ♥ 4 is now discarded from the open hand. The ♠ 9 is ducked to West who wins and plays a heart. A second spade is ducked to West, which completes our double ducking squeeze and rectifies the count for the last two tricks to be won on the board.

## The Suicide Squeeze

By definition a suicide squeeze is a squeeze inflicted upon one defender by his own partner. This can only happen by mistake or when declarer plays a card which loses to one defender and squeezes the other at the same time. A defender must actually win the squeeze trick if the definition is to apply.

### NORTH

♠ J3
♡ Q 10 4
◊ AKQ
♣ AQ652

WEST

♠ 852
♡ 752
◊ 94
♣ 10 9 8 7 3

EAST

♠ KQ 10 9 7
♡ 9863
◊ J 7 3 2
♣

### SOUTH

♠ A 6 4
♡ AKJ
◊ 10 8 6 5
♣ KJ4

The Auction:

| SOUTH | WEST | NORTH | EAST |
|-------|------|--------|------|
| 1 N.T. | Pass | 6 N.T. | Pass |
| Pass | Pass | | |

Opening Lead: ♣ 10

Declarer is all set to claim his small slam at Trick 1, until East fails to follow suit in clubs. His discard is the ♠10. Without a fifth club trick South can count only eleven sure winners. If the diamond suit splits three-three, or if the ♦ J is singleton or doubleton, a twelfth trick is available. But is there any possibility of a squeeze? There are several potential squeezes on this deal. West's hand may contain either the ♠ K Q or a four card diamond holding to go with his clubs, or East may be Busy in spades and diamonds. We should elect to play the spade-diamond Squeeze for two reasons: first, the ♠10 was a very emphatic signal as to the location of the missing spade honors, and second, four diamonds to our left leaves a highly unlikely distributional pattern to our right.

In working out our squeeze against East, L is out of order. To rectify the count we have two choices. A club trick can be lost to West, which is best, or a spade can be ducked out from under the ♠ A. This is not as good for it requires East to have started with six spades. Our ♠ 6 becomes the threat against East. Neither of these plays can succeed. Every squeeze ending requires that there be an entry into the hand which holds the single menace. If the ♦ 10 is our single menace, a spade return after we rectify the count removes our entry and destroys the squeeze.

The answer to our problem is a *suicide squeeze.*
East must be squeezed on the same trick used to rectify the count. The squeeze trick is a loser, not a winner. In this way your opponents cannot attack the spade entry to the South hand until after you rectify the count.

Here is the proper line of play. Declarer tries the diamond suit first. When the ♦ J fails to appear, three hearts are cashed and the club suit is run leaving this squeeze ending.

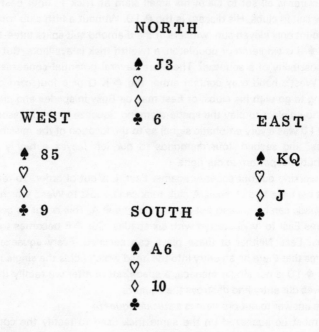

NORTH

♠ J3
♡
◇
♣ 6

WEST

♠ 85
♡
◇
♣ 9

EAST

♠ KQ
♡
◇ J
♣

SOUTH

♠ A6
♡
◇ 10
♣

North plays the ♣ 6, which is a loser, to West's squeeze card, the ♣ 9.
East is trapped in a Third Entry Form (Positional) squeeze.

South will hold whatever suit East discards. West must helplessly return a spade after he has taken the club.

## SUMMARY, CHAPTER V

From a declarer's point of view, there is very little left that you can learn about the single squeeze. You know how to unearth a possible squeeze that lies hidden in a complex combination of cards. You also know how to use squeeze techniques to avoid taking a finesse. The mark of a true bridge expert is how few finesses he takes, not how many.

Some of the squeeze situations, such as the suicide squeeze, the dual squeeze, and the cross-cross squeeze are very rare. Tuck them away in the back of your mind until that one time in a thousand when you can bring your knowledge to the fore and show the true metal of which you are made.

## Chapter VI

# Advanced Squeeze Problems

The problem hands in this chapter involve the advanced squeeze technology covered in the previous chapter. You are now going to work harder to come up with the winning sequence of plays that bring about the successful squeeze end position.

As before, you are shown the North-South hands plus the bidding and play to date. Think out each possible line of play based upon the ramifications of the information given. If you find you cannot solve the majority of these problems, don't worry. These are difficult problems and by simply browsing through the material you've just read in Chapter V, many problems will clarify themselves.

NORTH

♠ AJ10952
♡ 3
◊ A642
♣ 109

The Auction:

| SOUTH | WEST | NORTH | EAST |
|-------|------|-------|------|
| 1 ♡ | Pass | 1 ♠ | Pass |
| 2 N.T. | Pass | 3 ◊ | Pass |
| 4 N.T. | Pass | 5 ♡ | Pass |
| 6 N.T. | Pass | Pass | Pass |

SOUTH

♠ KQ
♡ AKQ10
◊ 853
♣ AJ84

Opening Lead: ◊ J

Trick 1: ◊J ?

Plan your play.

NORTH

♠ A J 10 9 5 2
♡ 3
♢ A 6 4 2
♣ 10 9

WEST                                    EAST

♠ 6                                      ♠ 8 7 4 3
♡ J 9 8 6 2                              ♡ 7 5 4
♢ J 10                                   ♢ K Q 9 7
♣ K Q 7 5 3          SOUTH               ♣ 6 2

♠ K Q
♡ A K Q 10
♢ 8 5 3
♣ A J 8 4

We will not draw the curtain of charity over South's auction. Not only did he bid 2 NT without a diamond stopper, he also barged into a small slam without being invited by his partner. Unfortunately, he went unpunished for his misdeeds.

West does well on defense to avoid giving declarer his twelfth trick on opening lead. South can count eleven winners: six spades, three hearts, and two minor suit Aces. The opening lead is allowed to hold, which rectifies the count. The continuation of the ♦ 10 is taken with dummy's ♦ A. Our contract seems to depend on the ♥ J. If it lies with East, a finesse would be successful. It could also fall under the ♥ A K Q. In addition, there are several squeeze possibilities.

The play to the first two tricks would lead us to believe that the ♦ K Q are located to our right. This gives us a possible red suit squeeze against RHO. There is also a chance for a minor suit squeeze if RHO holds the King-Queen of both suits. This is very remote, for it requires that too many cards be placed advantageously. Also, playing for this squeeze eliminates any opportunity for a squeeze against LHO in hearts and another suit.

West could possibly be squeezed in clubs and hearts. This also allows for a diamond-heart Squeeze against West at the same time. This either-or combination seems to offer the maximum number of possibilities on the hand.

Upon winning the ♦ A at. trick 2 we must first clear the ♣ A from the closed hand. Not only is this play necessary for our diamond-heart squeeze against East, but it is also a Vienna Coup for our heart-club squeeze against West. After the ♣ A, all the spades are played but one leaving this end situation.

```
                      NORTH

                      ♠ 5
                      ♡ 3
                      ◇ 64
     WEST             ♣ 10             EAST

     ♠                                 ♠
     ♡ J986                            ♡ 754
     ◇                                 ◇ KQ
     ♣ K        SOUTH                  ♣

                 ♠
                 ♡ AKQ10
                 ◇
                 ♣ J
```

Declarer leads the ♠5 from dummy and discards the ♣J from the closed hand. East has no difficulty finding a free discard. He is not squeezed. With est. it is a different story. He will undoubtedly pitch his ♥ 6 and hope his partner holds the ♥ Q.

Notice what happens if the ♣ A is not cashed before the spade suit is run. Neither squeeze will work even though the cards may be placed properly. This would be the end position.

NORTH

♠ 5
♡ 3
◇ 6 4
♣ 10 9

WEST                                              EAST

♠                                                 ♠
♡ J 9 8 6                                         ♡ 7 5 4
◇                                                 ◇ K Q
♣ K Q          SOUTH                              ♣ 6

♠
♡ A K Q 10
◇
♣ A J

Again North plays the ♠ 5 and pitches the ♣ J from the South hand. West now has a free discard in clubs. The ♣ 10 becomes a winner, but there is no entry to cash it. Try laying out the cards with the ♥ J in the Eust hand along with the ◆ K Q. This squeeze also fails if the ♣ A is not cleared before the count down. Now the right hand defender is left with an Idle card.

East missed his moment of greatness at Trick 1. If he had overtaken his partner's ◆ J and returned a heart, he would have destroyed condition E for the heart-club squeeze against West. Play the hand out for yourself with this defense and see.

**NORTH**

♠ 653
♡ J96
◇ 10653
♣ AJ9

**SOUTH**

♠ A94
♡ KQ1083
◇ AK
♣ K63

**The Auction:**

| NORTH | EAST | SOUTH | WEST |
|-------|------|-------|------|
| Pass | Pass | 1 ♡ | Pass |
| 2 ♡ | Pass | 4 ♡ | Pass |
| Pass | Pass | | |

**Opening Lead:** ◇ Q

Trick 1: ◇Q-3-2-A
Trick 2: ?

Plan your play.

# THE SIMPLE SQUEEZE IN BRIDGE

### NORTH

♠ 653
♡ J96
◊ 10653
♣ AJ9

### WEST

♠ Q10
♡ 74
◊ QJ98
♣ 108542

### EAST

♠ KJ872
♡ A52
◊ 742
♣ Q7

### SOUTH

♠ A94
♡ KQ1083
◊ AK
♣ K63

When playing this hand a novice bridge player pulls trump and finesses for the ♣ Q. Down one. The intermediate player ruffs out one of dummy's diamonds hoping for ♦ Q Jx in the West hand. When the diamond honors fail to fall, he too takes the club finesse. Down one. The bridge expert trumps out a diamond in much the same way as his intermediate counterpart, but he never takes the club finesse. The expert makes the hand by playing for a minor suit squeeze against LHO.

The cards should be played as follows. At Trick 2 declarer sets about the task of rectifying the count by playing the ♠ A and a small spade. East is likely to overtake his partner's ♠ Q and takes his second spade trick. If he doesn't, he can be forced to take it on the next round. A diamond return is won by the ♦ K, and the ♥ A is forced by playing small to the ♥ 9. If East continues a diamond it is ruffed in the closed hand. If the diamond is not returned, dummy is entered with a trump and the diamond is ruffed away. All the remaining hearts are played until this ending is reached.

# THE SIMPLE SQUEEZE IN BRIDGE

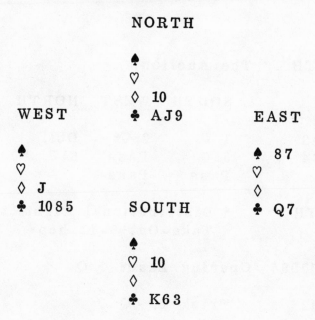

NORTH

♠

♡

◊ 10

♣ A J 9

WEST

♠

♡

◊ J

♣ 10 8 5

EAST

♠ 8 7

♡

◊

♣ Q 7

SOUTH

♠

♡ 10

◊

♣ K 6 3

South leads the last heart and West throws a club. The **D** 1 0 on board is now useless and can be discarded. Next comes the ♣ K and a small club. When the hand to your left fails to show up with the ♣ Q, dummy's ♣ A is played. The club finesse would be futile since West's last card is known to be the ♦ J. If West started with the ♣ Q, we have a squeeze. If not, East may have started with a doubleton ♣ Q, which becomes our little bonus for playing the hand as a squeeze.

NORTH        The Auction:

♠ A8         SOUTH    WEST    NORTH    EAST
♡ QJ3
◊ A843       1 ♡      2 ♡*    Dbl.     4 ♠
♣ K864       5 ♣      Pass    6 ♡      Pass
             Pass     Pass


SOUTH        * Distributional Light
               Take-Out 6-11 hcp
♠ J
♡ AK10986    Opening Lead: ◊ Q
◊ K6
♣ A532       Trick 1: ◊Q ?

Plan your play.

```
                        NORTH

                    ♠ A 8
                    ♡ Q J 3
                    ◇ A 8 4 3
        WEST        ♣ K 8 6 4        EAST

      ♠ K 9 5 2                      ♠ Q 10 7 6 4 3
      ♡ 4                            ♡ 7 5 2
      ◇ Q J 10 5                     ◇ 9 7 2
      ♣ Q J 9 7      SOUTH           ♣ 10

                    ♠ J
                    ♡ A K 10 9 8 6
                    ◇ K 6
                    ♣ A 5 3 2
```

East-West could have taken a profitable save by bidding 6 ♠ however, this is a difficult choice to make considering West's defensive values in the minor suits.

The opening lead is taken in the closed hand with the ♦ K, and trumps are drawn in three rounds. The success or failure of our contract would seem to depend upon how the outstanding clubs are arranged. Considering the distributional implications of West's 2 ♥ bid, there is reason to suspect that the suit may break badly. With this in mind we should look for some secondary play possibility to fall back on.

If West began this hand with four or more cards in each minor suit, he is a candidate for a squeeze. To set the stage for our squeeze play we must do three things: the ♠ A is to be cleared from dummy, a club trick must be lost to rectify the count, and a dimond needs to be ruffed to insure that West is the only opponent able to defend against the length card threat in the open hand.

Timing here is important. The ♠ A can go at any time, but the other two odd jobs must be performed in proper sequence. If we isolate the diamond menace and then rectify the count by condeding a club trick, we risk having

West win the club and play a fourth round of diamonds, which neatly disposes of our single menace.

After drawing trump the play should go as follows. A club is conceded to the enemy in a manner similar to a submarine squeeze. Declarer can handle any return. He wins each of his three remaining Aces: the ♣A, the ♠A, and the ♦A before ruffing a diamond to enter the closed hand. This is our three-card squeeze ending.

NORTH

♠
♡
♦ 8
♣ K8

WEST                              EAST

♠                                 ♠ Q 10 7
♡                                 ♡
♦ J                               ♦
♣ QJ          SOUTH               ♣

              ♠
              ♡ 10
              ♦
              ♣ 5 3

The last trump is led, and we await West's play.
He is caught in a Third Entry Form (Positional) squeeze.

# THE SIMPLE SQUEEZE IN BRIDGE

## NORTH

♠ J10952
♡ 10
◇ K103
♣ J952

## SOUTH

♠ 84
♡ AKQJ93
◇ AJ5
♣ A10

### The Auction:

| SOUTH | WEST | NORTH | EAST |
|-------|------|-------|------|
| 1 ♡   | Pass | 1 ♠   | Pass |
| 4 ♡   | Pass | Pass  | Pass |

Opening Lead: ♠ K

Trick 1: ♠K-2-6-4
Trick 2: ♡4 ?

Plan your play.

NORTH

♠ J 10 9 5 2
♡ 10
◇ K 10 3
♣ J 9 5 2

WEST

♠ K Q 7 3
♡ 8 5 4
◇ Q 7 4
♣ K 6 3

EAST

♠ A 6
♡ 7 6 2
◇ 9 8 6 2
♣ Q 8 7 4

SOUTH

♠ 8 4
♡ A K Q J 9 3
◇ A J 5
♣ A 10

There are nine easy winners on this hand, but what about the tenth? A diamond finesse can be taken, but in which direction? A finesse loses about half the time, and we would prefer not to take that chance.

The best play at Trick 3 is a small club toward the ♣ 10. If the ♣ K Q are to our right, we immediately manufacture a club winner. If not, we finesse the ♣ 10. This play creates a number of additional possibilities. It leaves a single club honor outstanding which must guard against the single threat left in dummy. East may have started with a doubleton club honor, or we may have succeeded in isolating a club honor for an eventual squeeze. The same thing is true in spades. The play of another round of the suit will force a second honor. This leaves the remaining high spade isolated against dummy's ♠ J. Now for the proper play.

A club finesse is taken to South's ♣ 10 at Trick 3. West wins the ♣ K. We can suspect the ♣ Q lies to our right. LHO leads another trump, which is as good as defense as anything else. South wins and plays another round. The remaining spade is led from the closed hand, which East must take with his ♠ A. We now know West has the ♠ Q. The theory of maximum pressure has just taken hold on RHO. Will he lead a club after seeing us take a finesse in the suit, or will he break the diamond suit for us? We have created an atmosphere in which he may make a mistake.

Let's assume East finds the correct play of a small club. The remaining hearts are played giving us t is end position with one trump left.

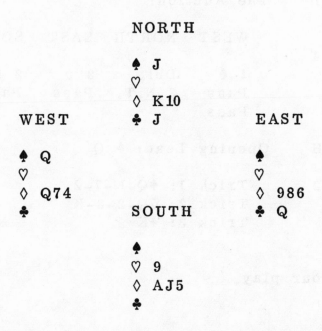

NORTH

♠ J
♡
◊ K 10
♣ J

WEST

♠ Q
♡
◊ Q 7 4
♣

EAST

♠
♡
◊ 9 8 6
♣ Q

SOUTH

♠
♡ 9
◊ A J 5
♣

South plays the ♥ 9. When West pitches a diamond, the ♠ J becomes worthless and can be released from dummy. East also pitches a diamond. A diamond is led to the ♦ K and the ♦ 10 is played from the board. South must make a decision. He knows that East has not been caught in a diamond-club squeeze when the ♦ Q did not show up at Trick 12. The question is, has West been squeezed in spades and diamonds, or did he false-card with the ♣ K holding ♣ K Q in which case, the diamond finesse works. This end position is unclear, but I personally would vote for split club honors, which makes a squeeze the better percentage play.

NORTH        The Auction:

♠ K63        WEST    NORTH    EAST    SOUTH
♡ QJ104
◇ KQ6        1 ♠     Dbl.     2 ◇     2 N.T.
♣ A64        Pass    3 N.T.   Pass    Pass
             Pass


SOUTH        Opening Lead: ♠ Q

♠ A1052      Trick 1: ♠Q-K-7-2
♡ 983        Trick 2: ♡Q-2-3-K
◇ A10        Trick 3: ♣K ?
♣ J952

Plan your play.

NORTH

♠ K63
♡ QJ104
◇ KQ6
♣ A64

WEST

♠ QJ984
♡ AK7
◇ 4
♣ KQ107

EAST

♠ 7
♡ 652
◇ J987532
♣ 83

SOUTH

♠ A1052
♡ 983
◇ A10
♣ J952

Declarer captures the opening lead with the ♠ K and immediately attacks the heart suit by playing the ♥ Q. West wins and plays the ♣ K, which he is allowed to hold. The loss of this trick plus the ♥ A K will bring declarer down to a lower count of two. Later in the hand he can decide whether to deliberatepy lose another trick, which rectifies the count for a squeeze, or leave the loser count as it is and play for squeeze throw-in.

LHO gets out with his singleton diamond, won by South's ♦ A. A heart continuation is won by West, who exists with a heart to avoid having to lead clubs or spades. It brings about this situation.

NORTH

♠ 6 3
♡ J
◊ KQ
♣ A 6

WEST

♠ J 9 8 4
♡
◊
♣ Q 10 7

EAST

♠
♡
◊ 9 8 7 5 3 2
♣ 8

SOUTH

♠ A 10 5
♡
◊ 10
♣ J 9 5

At this point it would be wrong for declarer to deliberately lose another trick in an attempt to rectify the count for a squeeze against LHO. North holds the upper hand on West and is without a threat. The only other possibility is to leave the loser count at two and try for a throw-in play. Declarer does not know that he could paly a small spade to West right now and he would be forced to return a spade or a club. Normally, South must play off the red suit winners in dummy to eliminate any possible exit cards from the hand to his left. By doing this we have a perfect picture of LHO's distribution. He started with four red cards and nine black ones. They must be five spades and four clubs. West would have opened the bidding 1 ♣ had the suit length been reversed.

As the red suit winners are played from the North hand it is necessary to count only one of West's black suits. This is the position with four cards remaining.

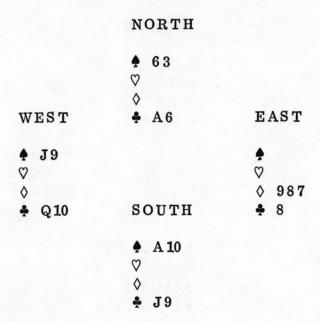

NORTH

♠ 6 3
♡
◊
♣ A 6

WEST

♠ J 9
♡
◊
♣ Q 10

EAST

♠
♡
◊ 9 8 7
♣ 8

SOUTH

♠ A 10
♡
◊
♣ J 9

Let's assume declarer has counted spades and knows that West still has two. This means his other two remaining cards must be clubs. The Ace of either black suit may be cashed and the suit continued to execute the throw-in. However, what happens if the opponent to the left tries to avoid the end-play by holding three spades? This leaves West with only one club, which must be the ♣ Q. Now the proper play is the ♣ A.

NORTH

&spades; A 9
&hearts; 10 8 6 5
&diams; K 9 5 2
&clubs; A Q 4

WEST

&spades; 10 5 2
&hearts; 7 3 2
&diams; 8 7 3
&clubs; 8 6 5 3

EAST

&spades; Q J 8 7
&hearts; K Q J 9
&diams; J 4
&clubs; K J 7

SOUTH

&spades; K 6 4 3
&hearts; A 4
&diams; A Q 10 6
&clubs; 10 9 2

You may remember this deal from Example (16) in Chapter III, but this time East did not double the final contract for a heart lead. West leads a club, and the play to the hand becomes correspondingly more difficult.

East wins the &clubs; J and shifts to the &hearts; K. Declarer allows the first heart to hold and wins a heart continuation with the &hearts; A. Four rounds of diamonds follow ending with the &diams; K in Dummy. Here is the situation before the last diamond is played.

# THE SIMPLE SQUEEZE IN BRIDGE

```
                    NORTH

                    ♠ A 9
                    ♡ 10 8
                    ◊ K
      WEST          ♣ A Q          EAST

      ♠ 10 5 2                     ♠ Q J 8
      ♡ 7                          ♡ J 9
      ◊                            ◊
      ♣ 8 6 5       SOUTH          ♣ K 7

                    ♠ K 6 4 3
                    ♡
                    ◊ 6
                    ♣ 10 9
```

The ◆ K Squeezes East. If he discards a heart, we can lead a heart from the North hand and give up a trick to gain one. This variation is similar to a squeeze Without the count. If RHO throws a spade, the ♠ K and ♠ A are cashed ending in dummy. The lead of a heart now end-plays East who is forced to lead clubs into our ♣ A Q.

If West had elected to lead the ♠ 2, the defense would fare no better. East is allowed to hold the lead. He can return either hearts or spades. It makes no difference. The end position will look like this.

### NORTH

♠
♡ 10 8
◇ K
♣ A Q

**WEST**

♠
♡ 7
◇
♣ 8 6 5 3

**EAST**

♠ Q
♡ Q J
◇
♣ K J

### SOUTH

♠ 6
♡
◇ 6
♣ 10 9 2

Again the lead of the ♦ K Squeezes East out of his setting trick before he is given the lead and eventually he will be forced to lead clubs.

# Chapter VII

# Defending Against A Squeeze

There is no substitute for paying attention on defense. You can learn all the systems, theorums, laws, and techniques you please, but if you fail to note what is occurring as a hand is being played, draw conclusions from what you see, and make assumptions upon which to base your defense, you will never ever become a competent bridge player.

Now that you have a basic knowledge of squeeze techniques, it is possible as a defender to see a squeeze being developed against yourself or your partner. Conceivably, something can be done to prevent the squeeze before it's too late.

Keep your eyes and your mind open. Take note not only of what declarer has bid and what he plays, but also of what he has not bid and what he has not played. Vigilance is the watchword of defense.

### Defending Against B, L, And E, But Not U

As a Declarer goes about the business of investigating the possibilities for a squeeze, he reviews the four conditions of BLUE and the four entry forms. When a possible squeeze is discovered, he undertakes the preliminary tasks such as isolating a menace, rectifying the count, etc. It is during this time period, as he is setting it up, that his squeeze is vulnerable to enemy attack.

Three of the four conditions of the BLUE Law, B, L, and E should receive your fullest attention, for they are subject to either aggressive attack or passive action on the part of the defense. It is usually impossible to defend against condition U. U is the equivalent of a fact of life. If it exists it exists, and nothing can be done about it.

As declarer considers the application of the BLUE Law against you or your partner, you should also review the same conditions against yourself. If a squeeze situation is found to exist, you should attempt to destroy one of declarer's three vulnerable conditions, B, L, or E. It may also be possible to defend against a squeeze by not making a play that assists the declarer in establishing his squeeze or by not discarding a card which throws your partner into a squeeze.

### Defending Against Condition B

There are two methods of defense against B. The first is to attack declarer's menaces, and the second is passive defense, whereby you protect as many of the outstanding suits for as long as you can. When one defender inadvertently gives up control of a suit and in so doing leaves his partner Busy in that suit plus another, a squeeze position may be caused to exist that was not there to begin with. More squeezes come through poor discarding on the part of the defense than in any other way.

### NORTH

- ♠ 8652
- ♡ 10
- ◇ K986
- ♣ K1042

### WEST

- ♠ KQJ9
- ♡ 742
- ◇ A73
- ♣ 987

### EAST

- ♠ 743
- ♡ QJ98
- ◇ 542
- ♣ QJ5

### SOUTH

- ♠ A10
- ♡ AK653
- ◇ QJ10
- ♣ A63

## The Auction:

| SOUTH | WEST | NORTH | EAST |
|-------|------|-------|------|
| 1 ♡ | Pass | 1 ♠ | Pass |
| 2 N.T. | Pass | 3 N.T. | Pass |
| Pass | Pass | | |

## Opening Lead: ♠ K

This is an example of passive defense. West gets off to a lead of the ♠ K. Declarer can take the first trick or hold off one round. It isn't going to make any difference. Diamonds are played and we, as West, are in with the ♦ A. We take our Spade tricks and watch as our partner makes one discard and our opponent makes two. Everyone plays hearts, the ♥ 8 from across the table, and the ♥ 5 3 from our right.* We should now get out with a diamond for fear that a club lead might give declarer a free finesse for the ♣ Q.

The moment of truth arrives as the fourth diamond is played from dummy. Here are the last six cards.

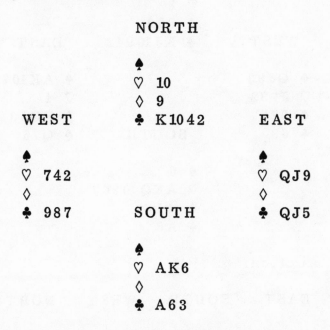

NORTH
♠
♡ 10
♢ 9
♣ K 10 4 2

WEST
♠
♡ 7 4 2
♢
♣ 9 8 7

EAST
♠
♡ Q J 9
♢
♣ Q J 5

SOUTH
♠
♡ A K 6
♢
♣ A 6 3

As North's ♦ 9 is played, East is forced to unguard hearts in order to defend against dummy's clubs. A club is released by the closed hand. Looking at all four hands the defense is easy, but when the South and East cards are hidden, West has a problem. We are unwilling to pitch a club for fear it will tip off the location of the ♣ Q if there is a two way finesse, and the ♥ 2 looks like such an insignificant card. Heart discards are the key to the defense of this hand. East would not have discarded the ♥ 8 and ♥ 9 if

*If your defensive partnership gives count, the H 9 would be played, planning to discard the H 8 to show an even number.

he held the ♥ 6. Declarer must have started with a five-card heart holding. South has actually played for a club-heart squeeze against your partner. He needed five hearts plus sole control of the club suit to be with East. The squeeze fails for lack of B. However, if West makes the mistake of releasing the lowly ♥ 2, the squeeze becomes a reality. Paying attention pays off!

### NORTH

♠ 854
♡ 8
◊ 862
♣ K J 10 9 4 2

### WEST

♠ Q J 9 3
♡ J 7 3 2
◊ 9 7 5
♣ 6 3

### EAST

♠ A K 10 7 2
♡ 4
◊ K Q J 3
♣ Q 7 5

### SOUTH

♠ 6
♡ A K Q 10 9 6 5
◊ A 10 4
♣ A 8

## The Auction:

| EAST | SOUTH | WEST | NORTH |
|------|-------|------|-------|
| 1 ♠ | Dbl. | 2 ♠ | 3 ♣ |
| 3 ♠ | 4 ♡ | Pass | Pass |
| Pass | | | |

## Opening Lead: ♠ Q

# THE SIMPLE SQUEEZE IN BRIDGE

As East you had better be on your toes at trick 1, or you may not beat this contract. If West's ♠ Q is allowed to hold, and he continues the suit, you have just let the hand get away from you.

Declarer will ruff the second spade and pull trump giving your partner his ♥ J. A diamond shift is now too late. South captures your diamond honor with the ♦ A and runs all his trump but one, which brings about this end position.

```
                    NORTH

                ♠
                ♡
                ◇ 8
                ♣ KJ10 9
   WEST                          EAST

 ♠ J                           ♠
 ♡                             ♡
 ◇ 97                          ◇ KQ
 ♣ 63          SOUTH           ♣ Q75

                ♠
                ♡ 6
                ◇ 10 4
                ♣ A 8
```

South plays his last heart and discards the diamond from the table. You are squeezed.

The pitch of a club gives declarer the rest of the tricks, so a diamond honor must go instead. The ♣ A followed by a diamond throw-in leaves you to lead clubs away from the ♣ Q.

This end-play could have been avoided. Sitting East you should have overtaken the ♠ Q and shifted to diamonds at Trick 2. By attacking the diamond menace before South has been able to rectify the count upsets declarer's time table, and the squeeze throw-in is averted.

NORTH

♠ 9853
♡ A52
◊ K32
♣ KQJ

WEST ♣

EAST

♠ KQJ102
♡ Q104
◊ QJ9
♣ A8

♠ 74
♡ 73
◊ 8754
♣ 97542

SOUTH

♠ A6
♡ KJ986
◊ A106
♣ 1063

The Auction:

| NORTH | EAST | SOUTH | WEST |
|-------|------|-------|------|
| 1 ♣ | Pass | 1 ♡ | 1 ♠ |
| Pass | Pass | Dbl. | Rdbl. |
| 2 ♡ | Pass | 4 ♡ | Pass |
| Pass | Pass | | |

Opening Lead: ♠ K

# THE SIMPLE SQUEEZE IN BRIDGE

South takes trick 1 with the ♠ A, crosses to the ♥ A on the board, and finesses trump, losing to your ♥ Q. After cashing a high spade, we stop to take stock of the situation.

South should have a five-card heart suit on this auction. With the two spades he has played he is left with six minor suit cards. If four of them are clubs, your partner will need the ♣ 10 to beat the hand, but south has three or more diamonds, you have a diamond trick coming to you that will beat this hand unless you let it get away.

Leading the ♦ Q looks very inviting, but it just has to be futile. According to the auction, your partner cannot possibly have the ♦ A. You could lead the suit once, but when you regain the lead with the ♣ A, diamonds become unplayable anytime South holds the ♦ 10.

If South holds the ♦ 10 it represents yet another problem. It means your partner cannot defend against the third round of the suit. We are Busy in two suits and can be set up for a spade-diamond squeeze. The play of the ♦ Q allows declarer to bring the hand down to the following end position.

```
                    NORTH

                    ♠ 9
                    ♡
                    ◊ K 3
        WEST        ♣              EAST

        ♠ J                        ♠
        ♡                          ♡
        ◊ J 9                      ◊ 8 7
        ♣              SOUTH       ♣ 9

                    ♠
                    ♡ 9
                    ◊ 10 6
                    ♣
```

By playing the ♥ 9 declarer gains a trick on a squeeze that could have been averted. We must attack the spade menace in dummy, and we must do it now, because both of North's little spades must be destroyed. If we, as West, play a high spade at Trick 4 and again when we regain the lead with the ♣ A, there can be no squeeze. Condition B will cease to exist.

## Defending Against L

Almost all squeezes operate when the declarer has reduced himself to a loser count of one. The exceptions to this are the squeeze throw-in, the squeeze without the count, and the losing squeeze trick. Therefore, it is possible to defeat an otherwise unbeatable contract by preventing declarer from rectifying the count. This is particularly true if the defender, who is refusing to win a particular trick, can do so and not give the situation away. A balk in the play may cause a knowledgeable opponent to convert his plan from a simple squeeze to a squeeze-throw-in or a squeeze without the count that is equally as effective.

### NORTH

♠ 10 8 4
♡ Q 8
◊ A Q 6 4
♣ K Q J 3

**WEST**

♠ A J 7 3
♡ 10 6 5 4
◊ J 10 7 2
♣ 2

**EAST**

♠ 9 5 2
♡ 9 7 3 2
◊ 9 5
♣ 8 7 5 4

### SOUTH

♠ K Q 6
♡ A K J
◊ K 8 3
♣ A 10 9 6

## The Auction:

| SOUTH | WEST | NORTH | EAST |
|-------|------|-------|------|
| 1 ♣ | Pass | 1 ◊ | Pass |
| 2 N.T. | Pass | 4 ♣ | Pass |
| 4 N.T. | Pass | 5 ◊ | Pass |
| 6 N.T. | Pass | Pass | Pass |

## Opening Lead: ♡ 4

# THE SIMPLE SQUEEZE IN BRIDGE

After the opening lead has been made and the dummy is tabled, it is a good defensive habit to stop for a moment and take stock of the situation. You would do well to ask yourself the following questions:

1) Is the dummy consistent with the auction?

2) Based upon the bidding plus what you see in your own hand and dummy, what do you think declarer and your partner have in their hands?

In answer to the first question the North hand is, if anything, slightly stronger than we might expect based upon his auction. South is known to hold about 19 hcp for his 2 NT rebid. When the ♥ J appears at Trick 1, his hand reads out like an open book. He must hold every missing high card not seen in your hand or lying on the table. You can expect no help from your partner on the defense of this contract.

There is one other fact that stands out. Declarer chose to play his contract at No Trump, not clubs, despite North's strong support. He is not likely to hold a five-card club suit.

With all of this information at your command it should be no problem for you, seated West, to review BLUE and see that you are about to become a candidate for a squeeze.

**Condition B.** Once we take our ♠ A, we will be Busy defending against dummy's ♠ 10 and the fourth diamond.

**Condition L.** Count declarer's winners. He has one spade, three hearts, three diamonds, and four clubs for a total of eleven tricks. This means that L is in good shape.

**Condition U.** Both the single threat of the ♠ 10 and the double threat in diamonds are with North, and North holds the Upper hand on you, seated West.

**Condition E.** The double threat in diamonds allows entry to the North hand.

To defeat a squeeze we must attack one of the conditions of the BLUE Law.

**Condition B.** There is no way partner can take over the defense of either Squeeze suit, nor can we destroy the spade or diamond threat.

**Condition L.** Declarer has eleven winners, but he has not rectified the count. This is a possible point of attack.

**Condition E.** With two honor cards in diamonds on the board plus the ♦ K in the closed hand, E is unassailable.

# THE SIMPLE SQUEEZE IN BRIDGE

At Trick 2 a spade is played from dummy and South plays the ♠ K. If we take the ♠ A, declarer wins any return, cashes all of his black suit winners and reduces the hand to this ending.

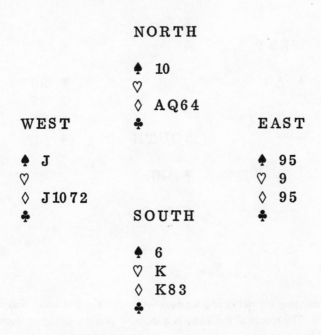

NORTH
♠ 10
♡
◇ A Q 6 4
♣

WEST
♠ J
♡
◇ J 10 7 2
♣

EAST
♠ 9 5
♡ 9
◇ 9 5
♣

SOUTH
♠ 6
♡ K
◇ K 8 3
♣

The play of the ♥ K squeezes us.

This didn't have to happen; not if the ♠ K was refused at Trick 2. In doing so we must be careful not to give the impression that we have the ♠ A. Declarer now has a problem. He may run his clubs before making a decision as to what to do next, but in the end he will either test the diamond suit or play another spade from dummy. The hand can then be beaten.

Now let's consider what happens if we refuse the spade trick but in doing so, we balk. Declarer is forewarned as to the location of the ♠ A. He runs the club suit and studies our discards intently. When we release two hearts and a spade, South knows it is safe to play his two remaining heart winners. Here is our situation as South plays his last heart.

**NORTH**

♠ 10 8
♡
♦ A Q 6 4
♣

**WEST**

♠ A J
♡
♦ J 10 7 2
♣

**EAST**

♠ 9 5
♡ 9 7
♦ 9 5
♣

**SOUTH**

♠ Q 6
♡ K
♦ K 8 3
♣

We become the victim of a squeeze without the count when South leads the ♥ K. The moral of the story is simple. If you are going to duck, duck smoothly.

### NORTH

- ♠ AQ84
- ♡ 865
- ◊ Q1098
- ♣ Q8

WEST

- ♠ 63
- ♡ QJ102
- ◊ A754
- ♣ 1052

EAST

- ♠ K1097
- ♡ 9743
- ◊ K
- ♣ J973

### SOUTH

- ♠ J52
- ♡ AK
- ◊ J632
- ♣ AK64

## The Auction:

| SOUTH | WEST | NORTH | EAST |
|-------|------|-------|------|
| 1 N.T. | Pass | 2 ♣ | Pass |
| 2 ◊ | Pass | 3 N.T. | Pass |
| Pass | Pass | Pass | |

## Opening Lead: ♡ Q

Our ♥ Q opening lead loses to South's ♥ A. The play of a diamond is taken by East's ♦ K, and his heart continuation goes to South's ♥ K. Another diamond is taken by us with the **D** A as our partner signals with the ♠10.

Normally it would be reflex action to cash the two heart winners we have worked so hard to set up and then lead a spade as our partner has requested, but look what pappens if we do. Declarer wins the ♠ A and leads diamonds. Here is the situation as the last two diamonds are being played.

                            NORTH

                            ♠ Q8
                            ♡
                            ◊ 10 9
            WEST            ♣ Q8            EAST

            ♠ 3                             ♠ K9
            ♡                               ♡
            ◊ 75                            ◊
            ♣ 10 5 2      SOUTH            ♣ J 9 7 3

                            ♠ J
                            ♡
                            ◊ 6
                            ♣ A K 6 4

It should not be too hard for us to work out BLUE for our partner's hand and see this squeeze coming based on the assumption he holds four clubs plus the ♠ K. Declarer takes his two diamond winners, and East is squeezed. He can afford to throw a spade on the first diamond, but the second one is fatal. What happens if we cash only one of our hearts before leading a spade? Now this would be our ending.

NORTH

♠ Q84
♡
◊ 109
♣ Q8

WEST

♠ 3
♡ 10
◊ 75
♣ 1052

EAST

♠ K9
♡ 9
◊
♣ J973

SOUTH

♠ J5
♡
◊ 6
♣ AK64

This time East is squeezed without the count. West has the ♠ 9 to use as a free discard on the first diamond, but then he must release his last heart in order to protect spades and clubs. The play of a spade after the squeeze sets up the ninth trick in the North hand. The only way for us to defeat this contract is to do the one thing that is completely contrary to our natrual instincts, and that is not to play hearts at all once they are set up. The lead of a spade forces declarer to win the ♠ A in the open hand. This is our end position as the diamond suit is played.

### NORTH

♠ Q 8 4
♡ 8
◇ 10 9
♣ Q 8

**WEST**

♠ 3
♡ J 10
◇ 7 5
♣ 10 5 2

**EAST**

♠ K 9
♡ 9 7
◇
♣ J 9 7 3

### SOUTH

♠ J 5
♡
◇ 6 3
♣ A K 6 4

Our partner must find two discards. As before, one of them is a spade, but there is now an extra heart in his hand to serve as a free discard that would not have been there if even one heart had been cashed.

What has happened here? By not cashing our heart winners, we have prevented Declarer from reaching a position with a loser count of one or two. A simple squeeze, a squeeze throw-in, or a squeeze Without the Count cannot be brought to bear against East as long as he has two hearts left, one to use as an exit card and the other to serve as an Idle discard.

### Defending Against E

Of the three conditions of BLUE that can be defended against, E is sometimes the easiest to attack and destroy. This is particularly true of the third and fourth entry forms involving split threats and blocked threats. You have only to look at some of the preceding examples and problem hands of these types to see that this is true. Split threats usually involve menaces. You should attack and destroy menace positions held against your partner by leading through them. They represent potential squeeze and squeeze throw-in positions. The lead through a tenace to break up a threat may be more important than leading a card to a sure winner in your partner's hand.

Of course each individual situation will dictate the proper action to be taken.

You should also watch for situations in which declarer has a limited number of entries to the dummy, or, less frequently, to his own hand. If the only entry or two entries to the open hand can be forced, your defense becomes much easier. All potential squeeze positions are automatically destroyed. One hand immediately becomes worthless and its cards need not be defended against. Declarer is required to make all of his plays away from his own holdings, which can be very advantageous to you, the defender.

```
                    NORTH

                    ♠ Q96
                    ♡ Q10
                    ♢ A85
        WEST        ♣ AK1053        EAST

    ♠ K743                          ♠ 85
    ♡ KJ6                           ♡ 87542
    ♢ Q                             ♢ 10972
    ♣ Q8762         SOUTH           ♣ J4

                    ♠ AJ102
                    ♡ A93
                    ♢ KJ643
                    ♣ 9
```

The Auction:

| NORTH | EAST | SOUTH | WEST |
|-------|------|-------|------|
| 1 ♣   | Pass | 1 ♢   | Pass |
| 2 ♣   | Pass | 3 N.T. | Pass |
| Pass  | Pass |       |      |

Opening Lead: ♠ 3

When playing match-point duplicate, it is just as important to prevent overtricks on defense as it is to make them as declarer. Quite often, the prevention of one overtrick will make the difference between an average plus and an average minus result on any given hand.

As West, you get off to a spade lead not knowing that, although North had bid and rebid clubs, the lead of that suit would have been more profitable. The ♠ 9 from dummy holds the trick. Declarer starts right in on the diamond suit. The ♦ A drops your ♦ Q. South wins two more diamonds before giving your partner a trick with the ♣ 10. East returns a spade and you are in with the ♠ K. The critical moment has arrived. If you play passively and get out with a spade, you will eventually be subjected to a club-heart squeeze. Not only that, but you should be able to see it coming.

Take a moment to consider the content of declarer's hand. He must have the ♥ A for his bid. This makes the ♥ Q a single menace against your ♥ K. With five clubs in your hand and five in dummy, do you really think your partner can defend against the suit? Clubs are a menace. You are about to become the victim of a first entry form (positional) squeeze if you don't do something about it right now. This will be the end position against you.

**NORTH**

♠
♡ Q
♦
♣ A K 10

**WEST**

♠
♡ K
♦
♣ Q 8 7

**EAST**

♠
♡ 8 7
♦
♣ J 4

**SOUTH**

♠
♡ 9 3
♦ 6
♣ 9

The play of the ♦ 6 will squeeze you, but there is a defense. You have no way to attack conditions B or L, but E offers some hope. If south started with only a singleton club, the lead of the suit will sever his lines of communication with the North hand. Condition E is thereby done away with and we are off the squeeze.

This deal is taken from an actual tournament event. Based on a twelve top, those East-West pairs that took three defensive tricks scored nine and one half match-points, while those pairs that managed only two defensive tricks received four and one half match-points. Because of the unique heart position on this hand, one declarer after another literally fell into a squeeze end position without any idea of what they were doing. You will notice that the ♥ A need not be cleared to uncover the ♥ Q as a single threat. This end position will work just as well.

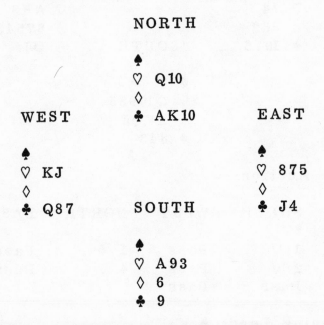

```
                       NORTH

                       ♠
                       ♡  Q 10
                       ◊
         WEST          ♣  A K 10          EAST

         ♠                                ♠
         ♡  K J                           ♡  8 7 5
         ◊                                ◊
         ♣  Q 8 7      SOUTH              ♣  J 4

                       ♠
                       ♡  A 9 3
                       ◊  6
                       ♣  9
```

As long as declarer discards a heart from the board as he leads his last diamond, he cannot go wrong on the play to the last five cards.

Before you can learn to defend against a squeeze, you must first be conversant with the basic tenets of defense. You must be able to collect information from the bidding, the play of the hand, and what you can see in your hand and in the dummy. Then plan a defensive course of action that stands a chance of defeating the contract or, if the contract is unbeatable, holding declarer to his minimum number of tricks.

NORTH

♠ QJ109
♡ J62
◇ 10
♣ AK952

WEST

♠ AK754
♡ 74
◇ 962
♣ 1076

EAST

♠ 632
♡ AK3
◇ 87543
♣ QJ

SOUTH

♠ 8
♡ Q10985
◇ AKQJ
♣ 843

## The Auction:

| SOUTH | WEST | NORTH | EAST |
|-------|------|-------|------|
| 1 ♡ | Pass | 1 ♠ | Pass |
| 2 ◇ | Pass | 4 ♡ | Pass |
| Pass | Pass | | |

## Opening Lead: ♠ K

On this hand we are seated in the East chair. Our partner has made an opening lead of the ♠ K on which we played the ♠ 2. He shifts to a heart and we are on lead with the ♥ K. Let's start by assembling all the information we know or can assume to be true about declarer's hand. There are only 12 hcps that we cannot locate. They must all be in the closed hand. With the ♦ A K Q J in the South hand, there is no need to clear the trump suit to prevent a ruff. South is sure to have a singleton spade. Dummy's club suit threatens to provide spade discards; therefore, partner would have cashed the ♠ A, but your play of the deuce indicated a holding of three and warned him off. Declarer's hand must be distributional. With only four-four in the red suits, he might have rebid 1 NT. If he has ten or more red cards, the hand is unbeatable. Our only hope is for five hearts and four diamonds. This gives us a club trick if West has three clubs headed by the ten.

Now that we have reached these conclusions, what can we do with the information? If our partner has the ♠ A plus three clubs to the ♣ 10, he is Busy in two suits and can be subjected to a squeeze. After the ♥ A K are forced out and trump is drawn, Declarer will run all of his diamonds and hearts but one, leaving this ending.

NORTH

♠ Q  
♡  
◊  
♣ AK9

WEST

♠ A  
♡  
◊  
♣ 10 7 6

EAST

♠ 6 3  
♡  
◊  
♣ QJ

SOUTH

♠  
♡ 8  
◊  
♣ 8 4 3

As he plays his last heart, our partner will be caught in a black suit squeeze. The time to prevent this from happening is at Trick 2 when we are first on lead with a trump. The loser count on the hand has not yet been reduced to one. We must resist the temptation to return a Spade trying to collect partner's ♠ A. To prevent the assumed squeeze, we must attack one of the conditions of BLUE now, while we still have another heart entry.

Dummy's ♣ A K provide entree to the North hand and both black threat suits. If they are forced off the board, the squeeze, if it exists, will fail for lack of E. We must lead a club at Trick 3 and again when we regain the lead with the ♥ A.

## SUMMARY, CHAPTER VII

As we have said before, vigilance is the watchword of the defense. If you pay attention and use the knowledge you have about the technical aspects of squeeze play plus the pointers included in this chapter, you should be able to foresee your opponent's squeeze like a storm brewing on the horizon. With adequate warning, you will often be able to plan a line of defense that will upset your adversaries' plans.

Chapter VIII

# Defensive Squeeze Problems

There is no law in the game of bridge that says the defenders must submit passively as declarer establishes and executes a squeeze against them. They are also not required to actively aid and abet declarer's cause although on some occasions you would think the defenders were really on the other team. Avoid making defensive plays that assist the enemy.

It will be unusual for you as a defender to have the opportunity to lead more than once or twice on any hand. Therefore, when you are on lead it is important that you make the most of it. All too often we have a tendency to make a play that gives nothing away. You cannot defend passively all the time. Depending upon the circumstances, you may be forced to make an attacking lead for the simple reason that inaction on your part leaves declarer with a sure-thing squeeze.

Study each defensive problem. You are shown your hand and the dummy. The auction and tricks played to date are also given. See if you can find the correct line of defense which destroys declarer's squeeze.

                          NORTH

                          ♠ K 10 9 6 3
                          ♡ 10 8
                          ◇ AK
            WEST          ♣ Q J 10 4

     ♠ 752
     ♡ 976532
     ◇ 73
     ♣ K3

The Auction:

     EAST      SOUTH      WEST       NORTH

     2 ◇*      Dbl.       Pass       3 ◇
     Pass      3 ♠        Pass       4 N.T.
     Pass      5 ♠        Pass       5 N.T.
     Pass      6 ♣        Pass       6 ♠
     Pass      Pass       Pass

     * Weak 2 Bid.

Opening Lead: ◇ 7

     Trick 1: ◇7-A-Q-2
     Trick 2: ♠3-8-A-2
     Trick 3: ♠Q-5-6 West ◇4
     Trick 4: ♠J-7-K West ◇5
     Trick 5: ♣10-2-6-K
     Trick 6: ?

Plan your defense.

**NORTH**

♠ K 10 9 6 3
♡ 10 8
◇ A K
♣ Q J 10 4

**WEST**

♠ 7 5 2
♡ 9 7 6 5 3 2
◇ 7 3
♣ K 3

**EAST**

♠ 8
♡ K Q
◇ Q J 10 9 5 4
♣ 8 7 5 2

**SOUTH**

♠ A Q J 4
♡ A J 4
◇ 8 6 2
♣ A 9 6

North-South bid their way directly to a small slam in spades after your partner opens a weak 2 bid in diamonds. What do you know about your partner's hand and the declarer's holding at the point you regain the lead at trick 5 with the ♣ K?

Partner started with a six-card diamond suit headed by the ◆ Q J 10. He had only one trump, which leaves him with six unknown cards in hearts and clubs. The opponent's Blackwood sequence told us East has no aces, but we do know he holds the ♥ K.

Declarer started with four spades and three small diamonds. He also has six unknown cards in hearts and clubs. By overtaking his ♠ J with dummy's ♠ K he left himself with an entry to the open hand. Is he setting up a squeeze against your partner with the trump suit established for use in the count down? Check out the BLUE Law for declarer.

**Condition B.** Declarer's third diamond is a single threat against East. You cannot defend the heart suit. If your partner holds only the ♥ K or the ♥ J the hand makes on a finesse, but if your partner holds the ♥ K Q or ♥ K Q J, he is Busy in the red suits.

**Condition L.** Count declarer's winners. He has five spades, the ♥ A, two diamonds, and three clubs for a total of eleven winners. Your ♣ K rectifies the count.

**Condition U.** South holds the Upper hand on East. He has the single threat in the form of the third diamond. The heart suit provides either a double threat or a split threat, depending on the location of the ♥ J. In either case, condition U is satisfied.

**Condition E.** If Declarer cashes all of his clubs and diamonds before running trump, the fifth spade in the open hand will be the squeeze card for either a first or third entry Form (Positional) squeeze against partner! 

To break the squeeze you must attack one of the vulnerable conditions of BLUE. Nothing can be done with B or L, but what about E? Here we have the answer. Declarer must have an entry to the South hand after he has played his squeeze card. Without it the threats in the Upper hand are worthless. Let's look at the remaining cards.

```
                    NORTH

                    ♠  10 9
                    ♡  10 8
                    ◊  K
      WEST          ♣  J 10 4          EAST

      ♠                                ♠
      ♡  976532                        ♡  K Q
      ◊  3                             ◊  J 10 9 5
      ♣  3               SOUTH         ♣  8 7

                        ♠  4
                        ♡  A J 4
                        ◊  8 6
                        ♣  A 9
```

We must lead a heart in the hopes our partner has the ♥ K Q. This attacks condition E and destroys the squeeze. Play the hand out from this point with and without a heart lead at Trick 6, and you will see that the heart menace will no longer be a threat because the South hand will be entryless after the clubs are run.

### NORTH

♠ KQJ6
♡ AJ
♢ AQ10 2
♣ J94

### EAST

♠ 8752
♡ Q7
♢ J963
♣ Q10 2

The Auction:

| SOUTH | WEST | NORTH | EAST |
|-------|------|-------|------|
| 1 N.T. | Pass | 2 ♣ | Pass |
| 2 ♠ | Pass | 4 N.T. | Pass |
| 5 ♡ | Pass | 5 N.T. | Pass |
| 6 ♠ | Pass | 7 ♠ | Pass |
| Pass | Pass | | |

Opening Lead: ♡ 10

Trick 1: ♡10-J-Q-K
Trick 2: ♠4-3-K-2
Trick 3: ♠Q-5-9 West ♡2
Trick 4: ♡A-7-3-4
Trick 5: ♠6-7-10 West ♡5
Trick 6: ♡6-8 North ♠J ?

Plan your defense.

### NORTH

♠ KQJ6
♡ AJ
◊ AQ102
♣ J94

|        WEST        |                    |        EAST        |
|--------------------|--------------------|--------------------|

WEST

♠ 3
♡ 1098542
◊ 754
♣ 873

### SOUTH

EAST

♠ 8752
♡ Q7
◊ J963
♣ Q102

### SOUTH

♠ A1094
♡ K63
◊ K8
♣ AK65

It is part of a bridge player's natural instinct for survival to hoard trumps. This hand serves to illustrate the fact that it may become necessary to discard your trump in order to keep from being squeezed.

North decides to "shoot for the moon" and bids a grand slam once he is sure there are no missing aces or kings. The heart lead loses to South's ♥ K followed by two high trump from the board, which reveals the bad trump split. Declarer discontinues spades in favor of the ♥ A. He returns to his hand with the ♠ 10 in order to ruff his last heart in the open hand. As East you must find a free discard.

South's bid of 6 ♠ places him with the ♦ K. It is obvious that a diamond discard would give away a trick. On instinct the tendency would be to keep our remaining trump and throw what seems to be a worthless card, the lowly ♣ 2. This would turn out to be a very expensive mistake. You are unnecessarily submitting to a squeeze in order to hold your last trump, which is actually nothing more than an Idle card. You can be sure that once declarer has ruffed this heart he is going to return to his hand and take your last trump away from you.

The winning defense is to underruff at trick 6. By using your last trump as a free discard, you avoid having to give up your tenace of ♣ Q 10 2 over the ♣ J 9 4 on the board. This is what the last seven cards would look like.

NORTH

♠ 532
♡ KQ54
◇ A4
♣ 9643

WEST

♠ 74
♡ J87
◇ KJ8
♣ AK1082

The Auction:

| SOUTH | WEST | NORTH | EAST |
|-------|------|-------|------|
| 1 ♠* | 2 ♣ | 3 ♠** | Pass |
| 4 N.T. | Pass | 5 ◇ | Pass |
| 6 ♠ | Pass | Pass | Pass |

\* Five-Card Majors.
** Limit raise.

Opening Lead: ♣ K

Trick 1: ♣K-3-Q-5
Trick 2: ?

Plan your defense.

NORTH

♠ 5 3 2
♡ K Q 5 4
◊ A 4
♣ 9 6 4 3

WEST                                        EAST

♠ 7 4                                        ♠ Q
♡ J 8 7                                      ♡ 9 6 3 2
◊ K J 8                                      ◊ 9 7 6 5 3
♣ A K 10 8 2        SOUTH                    ♣ Q J 7

♠ A K J 10 9 8 6
♡ A 10
◊ Q 10 2
♣ 5

All too often in a hand of this type it is reflex action for West to continue with a second club at Trick 2 because it looks safe. This is nothing less than a sign of mental laziness, for it is that play which allows declarer to fulfill his contract.

As West, your club continuation is trumped by South. Trumps are drawn in two rounds followed by three top hearts ending in dummy. A small diamond is released from the closed hand. Another club is ruffed by South, and the balance of the spade suit is played. Here is the situation with one trump remaining.

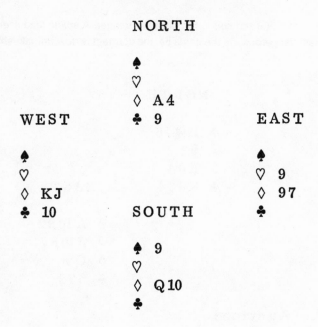

NORTH

♠
♡
◊ A 4
♣ 9

WEST

♠
♡
◊ KJ
♣ 10

EAST

♠
♡ 9
◊ 97
♣

SOUTH

♠ 9
♡
◊ Q 10
♣

You are squeezed by the play of declarer's last spade in an end position that you should have foreseen and avoided if you had only taken the time to think at trick 2.

After winning the opening lead, you should have considered the situation more closely. Regardless of what your opinion is of North's limit raise, Declarer could not possibly have bid this small slam holding a doubleton worthless club. You know a club continuation is going to be trumped. The suit should not be continued just because it represents a convenient exit from your hand. You must consider the ramifications.

If South holds three hearts headed by the ace, the suit sets up and we probably aren't going to beat this contract; therefore, we must play South for a doubleton. This leaves the ♦ A and a heart as the only two entries to dummy. If the ♦ Q is in the closed hand, a club-diamond squeeze can be negotiated against you providing the club threat can be isolated. Don't assist declarer in isolating the club menace against yourself by continuing the suit at Trick 2. To isolate the menace for himself, declarer needs two entries to the North hand to ruff clubs plus a third entry to satisfy E for his squeeze. If he doesn't have three hearts, he doesn't have the third entry to dummy.

The play of either red suit is fraught with danger. A spade lead seems to be the least dangerous. As the cards lie, the contract is now unmakeable.


### NORTH

♠ KQJ6
♡ 93
◇ K64
♣ KJ64     **EAST**

         ♠ A1092
         ♡ J1087
         ◇ Q9
         ♣ 532

## The Auction:

| SOUTH | WEST | NORTH | EAST |
|-------|------|-------|------|
| 1 ♡* | Pass | 1 ♠ | Pass |
| 2 N.T. | Pass | 4 N.T. | Pass |
| 6 N.T. | Pass | Pass | Pass |

* Five-Card Majors.

Opening Lead: ♣ 10

Trick 1: ♣10–4–2–A
Trick 2: ♠4–3–K ?

## Plan your defense.

## Chapter IX

# The Defenders Squeeze Declarer

It is not uncommon to see declarer play his cards in such a way as to squeeze himself. It is uncommon to see his opponents play their cards in such a way as to squeeze the declarer.

If you read to any great extent what has been written about squeeze play, you will be left with the definite impression that all squeezes are the exclusive property of the declarer. This is not so. Although they will not occur with nearly the same frequency as a declarer squeeze, it is possible for two defenders to gang up on one of their opponents and apply a squeeze against either the dummy or the closed hand.

The ability of one partnership to execute a squeeze against the other is directly related to the total number of high card points held between the two hands. There are more declarer squeezes in slam contracts than in game contracts. Therefore, it follows that more squeezes occur when bidding game than in part score situations.

The direct opposite is true of defender squeezes. There is no chance of the defenders executing a squeeze against a slam. Very few defensive squeezes occur at game contracts. It is in part score situations and in particular when defending 1 NT that most defensive squeezes take place. This is more likely to be true when all of the offensive high card strength is located in one hand, while the other is almost completely valueless. For this same reason, most of the defender squeezes that come to pass are of the squeeze throw-in or squeeze without the count variety.

# Developing BLUE Against Declarer

It is much more difficult for the defense to check out the conditions of the BLUE law and execute a squeeze with the same exactness as declarer. This is due to the inability of the defenders to see each others hand in the same way declarer can view his own hand and the Dummy. But occasionally it can be done.

## NORTH

♠ 10 9 8 6 3
♡ 8 2
◇ A Q 10
♣ 6 3 2

WEST

♠ Q J 7 4
♡ K 6 3
◇ 4 2
♣ A Q 8 7

EAST

♠ K 5 2
♡ A 10 9 7 4
◇ J 9 8 7
♣ 4

SOUTH

♠ A
♡ Q J 5
◇ K 6 5 3
♣ K J 10 9 5

The Auction:

| EAST | SOUTH | WEST | NORTH |
|------|-------|------|-------|
| Pass | 1 ♣ | Pass | 1 ♠ |
| 2 ♣* | Dbl. | 2 ♡ | Pass |
| Pass | Dbl. | Pass | 2 ♠ |
| Pass | 2 N.T. | Dbl. | Pass |
| Pass | Pass | | |

* Distributional Light
Take-Out 6-11 hcp

Opening Lead: ◇ 4

Declarer goes wrong on this hand when he uses up his diamond stoppers as entries to dummy to take repeated club finesses that cannot succeed based upon the auction. The opening lead is taken with the ♦ K in the closed hand, and the dummy is entered with the ♦ Q. A club finesse is taken to the **C** 9, which West allows to hold. The open hand is re-entered with the ♦ /♣ and another club is led. East signals with the ♥ 10 as West wins the trick with the ♣ Q.

West should have a fairly accurate picture of his partner's hand after the play to the first five tricks. East should have the ♥A, the ♦ 9, and a spade honor, probably the ♠ K. By reviewing the BLUE Law, West comes up with the following.

**Condition B.** The closed hand holds two high clubs. One of them must be held to defend against West's ♣ 8. If East has the ♥ A, as the discard of the ♥ 10 would seem to indicate, the heart suit can be used as a double threat regardless of what South holds in the suit.

**Condition L.** Five tricks have been played. There are eight remaining. After the play of a small spade, which rectifies the count, West will be able to count six defensive winners out of the seven tricks left. These are, two spades, two hearts, the ♦ 9, and the ♣ A. This sets the stage for a club-heart squeeze against the South hand.

West leads a small Spade. South takes East's ♠ K with the ♠ A and leads the ♣ K. West wins the ♣ A and plays two rounds of high spades on which Declarer discards his last diamond and a small club, bringing about this position.

NORTH

♠ 10 9
♡ 8 2
♢
♣

WEST

♠
♡ K 6 3
♢
♣ 8

EAST

♠
♡ A 9 7
♢ 9
♣

SOUTH

♠
♡ Q J 5
♢
♣ J

West leads a small heart to his partner's ace. East plays the ♦ 9 and squeezes South in hearts and clubs for down three and plus 800 points to the defense.

### NORTH

♠ A952
♡ 853
◊ 963
♣ 1086

### WEST

♠ 8
♡ QJ104
◊ 107542
♣ A73

### EAST

♠ J1073
♡ 9762
◊ 8
♣ KJ52

### SOUTH

♠ KQ64
♡ AK
◊ AKQJ
♣ Q94

## The Auction:

| SOUTH | WEST | NORTH | EAST |
|-------|------|-------|------|
| 2 N.T. | Pass | 3 ♣ | Pass |
| 3 ♠ | Pass | 4 ♠ | Pass |
| Pass | Pass | | |

Opening Lead: ♡ Q

South takes Trick 1 with the ♥ A and plays the ♠ K Q. He now knows that East started with four trumps. The second high heart is cashed and declarer crosses to dummy with the ♠ A. A heart is ruffed with South's remaining spade. As the diamond suit is played, East refuses to ruff at his first opportunity. He elects to use his ♠ J on the third round, just as the last diamond in dummy is played. This hold-up play rectifies the count for the squeeze in addition to depriving declarer of a diamond entry to the closed hand. Here is the situation before the last heart is played.

East plays his remaining heart and South becomes the victim of a suicide squeeze. The ♥ 9 can be ruffed in dummy, but in the process South must relinquish control of a minor suit. Even though the club finesse would win, declarer cannot retain enough cards to protect both clubs and diamonds.

NORTH

♠ Q10652
♡ 653
◇ 105
♣ 543

WEST

♠ 98
♡ AK8
◇ 862
♣ A10872

EAST

♠ KJ7
♡ 972
◇ AJ743
♣ 96

SOUTH

♠ A43
♡ QJ104
◇ KQ9
♣ KQJ

The Auction:

| SOUTH | WEST | NORTH | EAST |
|-------|------|-------|------|
| 1 N.T. | Pass | Pass | Pass |

Opening Lead: ♣ 7

# THE SIMPLE SQUEEZE IN BRIDGE

On this deal, North-South reach an inferior score of 1 NT. 2 ♠ would have been a better contract. The opening lead is won in the closed hand, and the ♠ A and a small spade are played in an attempt to set up dummy's long suit. East wins and should cash his other high spade. This is done to prevent declarer from using his spade late in the hand as either a throw-in or as a free discard. It is good procedure defensively as well as offensively to remove idle cards from your opponent's hand whenever possible.

East now returns his partner's suit, clubs. West wins and continues to clear the suit. South takes the club and plays a high heart. West is in again and starts to run the balance of the club suit. This is the position before the last club is played.

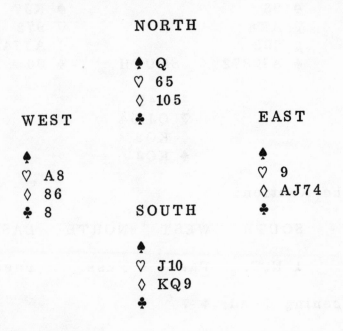

NORTH

♠ Q
♡ 6 5
◇ 10 5
♣

WEST

♠
♡ A 8
◇ 8 6
♣ 8

EAST

♠
♡ 9
◇ A J 7 4
♣

SOUTH

♠
♡ J 10
◇ K Q 9
♣

East discards the ♦ 4.
South is squeezed.

He must part with the ♦ 9. It is most important that East realize what has happened so that when his partner plays a diamond, he ducks the trick. South has been the victim of a squeeze without a count, but it will do no good if East carelessly wins the ♦ A in order to put another heart through the closed hand. By ducking he insures taking the balance of the tricks for down three and plus 300.

Throughout this entire discussion please do not fail to take note of the key play that made this squeeze possible. If East had not had the foresight to clear the ♠ K, our ending would have looked like this.

<pre>
                         NORTH

                      ♠  Q 6
                      ♡  6 5
                      ◊  10 5
         WEST         ♣              EAST

    ♠                               ♠  K
    ♡  A 8                          ♡  9
    ◊  8 6 2                        ◊  A J 7 4
    ♣  8            SOUTH           ♣

                      ♠  4
                      ♡  J 10
                      ◊  K Q 9
                      ♣
</pre>

South now has an Idle card to throw on the last club, and he is off the squeeze. In a rubber bridge game the difference between plus 200 and plus 300 above the line is not terribly significant, but at duplicate it can be the difference between just another good score and a cold top.

NORTH

♠ J 10 8 4 2
♡ AK 5 2
◇ 6 4
♣ A 6

WEST

♠ A 5
♡ 10
◇ AQJ 7 2
♣ Q 9 7 4 3

The Auction:

| WEST | NORTH | EAST | SOUTH |
|------|-------|------|--------|
| 1 ◇ | Dbl. | Pass | 1 N.T. |
| Pass | Pass | Pass | |

Opening Lead: ♣ 4

Trick 1: ♣4 – 6 – 8 – J
Trick 2: ♡3 – 10 – A – 4
Trick 3: ♡K – 7 – 6 West ♣3
Trick 4: ♣A – 2 – 10 – 4
Trick 5: ♡2 – Q – 9 ?

Plan your defense.

### NORTH

- ♠ J 10 8 4 2
- ♡ A K 5 2
- ◇ 6 4
- ♣ A 6

### WEST

- ♠ A 5
- ♡ 10
- ◇ A Q J 7 2
- ♣ Q 9 7 4 3

### EAST

- ♠ K Q 9 7
- ♡ Q 8 7 4
- ◇ 8 5
- ♣ 8 5 2

### SOUTH

- ♠ 6 3
- ♡ J 9 6 3
- ◇ K 10 9 3
- ♣ K J 10

South makes an unfortunate choice when he elects to bid 1 NT because of his strong diamond position rather than 1 ♥ on a weak four card holding.

The ♣ J takes trick 1 in the closed hand. A small heart is played to dummy's ACE as LHO contributes the ♥ 10. Declarer is encouraged to cash the ♥ K in hopes of dropping a doubleton ♥ Q from the West hand. When this fails to materialize, the ♣ A is cleared before playing another heart. At this point, as West you should be able to see the squeeze.

South is known to hold four hearts and three clubs. The remaining spades and diamonds are most likely four-two in favor of diamonds. The most important piece of information you have comes from something that did not happen, rather than something that did. Declarer did not attack the most obvious suit in dummy as a source of tricks. He therefore, does not have either the ♠ K or ♠ Q. This makes the ♠ K in your partner's hand a potential squeeze card.

East wins the ♥ Q and leads a diamond. As West, we have been forced to find two discards as the hearts were played. They were one each from our two five-card suits. We take the diamond with the ♦ J and play the ♠ A and another spade to partner's ♠ Q.

Here is the position at trick 9 with West to lead.

### NORTH

♠ J84
♡ 5
◇ 6
♣

WEST ♣ EAST

♠                         ♠ K9
♡                         ♡ 8
◇ AQ7              ◇ 5
♣ Q9       SOUTH       ♣ 8

♠
♡ J
◇ K10 3
♣ K

Partner leads his ♠ K, and declarer is squeezed. He cannot part with the ♥ J, or East will play the ♥ 8 and the squeeze will repeat itself. If he throws the ♣ K, West will pitch the ♦ 7 and win the last four tricks when East leads his remaining diamond. This leaves South only one choice; to pitch a diamond. West now eliminates a club from his hand and takes three more diamond tricks before surrendering the last club to declarer.

Any time you defeat 1 NT two tricks on a squeeze for plus 200 and a top match-point result, you may be justly proud of a result that few pairs will achieve.

NORTH

♠ J4
♡ 532
♢ AQ84
♣ 6532

WEST

♠ K1097
♡ A964
♢ J3
♣ KQ10

The Auction:

| SOUTH | WEST | NORTH | EAST |
|-------|------|-------|------|
| 1 ♢ | Dbl. | 2 ♢ | 2 ♠ |
| 2 N.T. | Pass | 3 N.T. | Pass |
| Pass | Pass | | |

Opening Lead: ♣ K

Trick 1: ♣K–2–9–8
Trick 2: ♣Q–3–4–A
Trick 3: ♢2–3–A–7
Trick 4: ♢Q–5–J East ♠2
Trick 5: ♢4–K East ♠3 West ♠7
Trick 6: ♢10–8 East ♠5 West ♡4
Trick 7: ♢9 East ♠6 West ♠9 North ♣5
Trick 8: ♢6 ?

Plan your defense.

### NORTH

♠ J 4
♡ 5 3 2
◊ A Q 8 4
♣ 6 5 3 2

### WEST

♠ K 10 9 7
♡ A 9 6 4
◊ J 3
♣ K Q 10

### EAST

♠ 8 6 5 3 2
♡ K 8 7
◊ 7
♣ J 9 7 4

### SOUTH

♠ A Q
♡ Q J 10
◊ K 10 9 6 5 2
♣ A 8

As West, you lead the ♣ K and are allowed to hold the first trick. Your partner's play is the ♣ 9, which by agreement is his second best card in the suit. This places him possibly with the C A, but more likely the ♣ J. South wins Trick 2 by taking our ♣ Q with the ♣ A and begins to run his diamond winners. When East fails to follow to the second diamond, we know that declarer has a six-card suit. We must find four discards. The first three are easy, two spades and a heart, but what shall we throw to Trick 8?

Partner has pitched three small spades indicating a disinterest in the suit and placing the ♠ A Q in the closed hand. We have also seen the ♣ A and the ♦ K by declarer. This leaves only the ♥ K Q J unaccounted for. Our partner must hold at least the ♥ K for his bid of 2 ♠ Knowing all of this, what can we expect declarer's next play to be?

Since most declarers believe that discretion is *not* the better part of valour, it is doubtful that South is going to cash his ♠ A and settle for down one. It isn't likely that declarer has a club to play. If he had a third club, he would have held off another round in the hope of setting up a long suit winner in dummy. He is almost sure to lead a heart and try for an end-play in spades.

# THE SIMPLE SQUEEZE IN BRIDGE

If declarer's major suit holdings resemble ♠ A Q and ♥ J 10, our proper discard is the ♣ 10, not a heart.    We need our ♥ 6 as part of our double threat to squeeze declarer. This is what the end position will be with five cards to play.

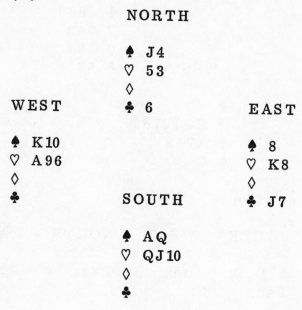

NORTH

♠ J4
♡ 53
◇
♣ 6

WEST

♠ K10
♡ A96
◇
♣

EAST

♠ 8
♡ K8
◇
♣ J7

SOUTH

♠ AQ
♡ QJ10
◇
♣

Declarer's play of the ♥ Q is won by East, who now cashes his two club winners. The ♠ K is our single threat and the ♥ A 9 is our double threat. You can now see the importance of keeping the ♥ 6 in favor of the ♣ 10.

Much to his horror and embarrassment, South finds himself squeezed by East's club plays. He can afford to throw the ♠ Q on the first one, but the second club administers the kiss of death. Declarer is squeezed out of his heart stopper or his ♠ A for down two.

South could have tried playing hearts before the last diamond, but the result would have been the same. He is now forced to give up the diamond and the ♠ Q to protect both major suits. A spade lead by East gives us the last two tricks with the ♥ A and the ♠ K. Try this line of play for yourself, and observe the helplessness of the poor suffering declarer.

NORTH

♠ J863
♡ 542
◊ J84
♣ 653

WEST

♠ K
♡ KQJ9763
◊ A752
♣ Q

The Auction:

| SOUTH | WEST | NORTH | EAST |
|-------|------|-------|------|
| 1 N.T. | Dbl. | Pass | Pass |
| Pass | | | |

Opening Lead: ♡ K

Trick 1: ♡K–2–8–A
Trick 2: ◊3–2–J–6
Trick 3: ◊4–9 East ♣9 ?

Plan your defense.

### NORTH

♠ J863
♡ 542
◊ J84
♣ 653

### WEST

♠ K
♡ KQJ9763
◊ A752
♣ Q

### EAST

♠ Q10754
♡ 8
◊ 6
♣ A98742

### SOUTH

♠ A92
♡ A10
◊ KQ10093
♣ KJ10

As West, we know by Trick 3 that South started with the ♥ A and the ♦ K as part of his 16-18 hcp. If the balance of his hand is the ♠ A and the ♣ K, he is Busy in two suits.

As West we have the upper hand on South. Our ♠ K and ♦ 7 are both single threats against our right hand opponent.

If East's play of the ♣ 9 indicates that he has the ♣ A, we can use the club suit as a double menace as long as partner has a spot-card higher than dummy's ♣6.

Our only problem is the loser count. If we hold up one round of diamonds and then take our ♦ A, we can cash all of our hearts and force South to come down to a three-card ending. He won't be able to hold onto the ♠A along with a high diamond and still be able to protect the ♣ K. Here are the last four cards with West about to apply the coup de-gras.

NORTH

♠ J 8
♡
◊
♣ 6 5

WEST

♠ K
♡ 3
◊ 7
♣ Q

EAST

♠
♡
◊
♣ A 8 7 4

SOUTH

♠ A
♡
◊ K
♣ K J

West's play of the ♥ 3 catches South in a three suit repeating squeeze. If he discards a club, East can win the balance of the tricks by overtaking West's ♣ Q. If instead, he throws a diamond or a spade, West now has a winner in that suit and re-applies the squeeze.

## SUMMARY, CHAPTER IX

The development of a squeeze by the defenders against declarer's hand or the dummy is a subject about which very little has been written. The infrequency with which such a squeeze takes place limits the time and space that can be devoted to the subject.

While defending, keep your eyes, ears, and mind open to the possibility of finding one hand with the majority of the offensive high cards. Then see what pressure can be brought to bear by applying BLUE.

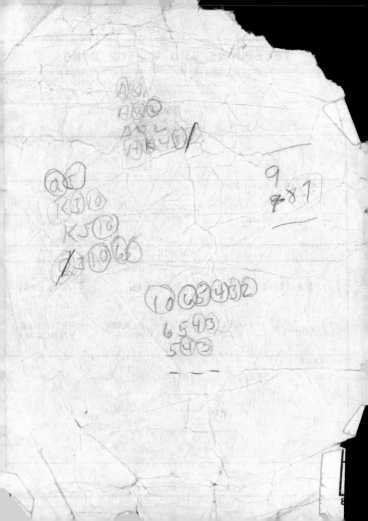

# TELEPHONE AND VISITOR MEMO.

| TIME | DATE |
|---|---|

**CALLER**

**OFFICE OR ORGANIZATION**

| TELEPHONE NUMBER | EXTENSION |
|---|---|

## CHECK

☐ IS WAITING     ☐ WILL RETURN     ☐ WAS HERE

☐ PHONED    ☐ WILL PHONE AGAIN    ☐ PLEASE PHONE    ☐ RETURNED YOUR CALL

**MESSAGE**

**SIGNATURE**

2-S-4 (Rev. 3/61)

# EPILOGUE

Now that you have completed this book, I hope you feel that you have come a long way toward improving your card playing abilities both as a declarer and defender. Adding a complete understanding of the single squeeze to your arsenal of bridge weaponry is certainly a giant step in the right direction, but don't stop here.

You have only just begun to scratch the surface when it comes to the squeeze and other end-play techniques. If you put this book aside and go no further, you do yourself a disservice. Keep it available to refresh yourself and to review those areas in which you are not quite that proficient. You should also read further with other authors to increase your knowledge about advanced squeeze and end-play techniques.

To prove to you that there are still vast horizons out there for you to conquer, I leave you with just one more squeeze problem to solve. With the benefit of being able to see all four hands, can you make 7 ♠ on this deal against best defense? The opening lead is the ♣ Q.

## NORTH

♠ A K
♡ A Q 2
♢ A Q 2
♣ A K 4 3 2

**WEST**

♠ Q J
♡ K J 10
♢ K J 10
♣ Q J 10 6 5

**EAST**

♠ 9 8 7
♡ 9 8 7
♢ 9 8 7 6
♣ 9 8 7

## SOUTH

♠ 10 6 5 4 3 2
♡ 6 5 4 3
♢ 5 4 3
♣